Narcissism

The Self-Centered Personality Exposed

2nd Edition

by Jeffery Dawson

Legal Notice:

Disclaimer Notice:

CONTENTS

Introduction

Pride, arrogance, ego, and admiration; these are all feelings that are okay in moderation. However, a narcissist is overly proud, egotistical and thinks that they are entitled to everything they want. So, what really is narcissism?

Narcissism has its roots in Greek mythology, when a young man named Narcissus fell in love with a water pool reflection of himself. Narcissus was a Greek hunter from Boeotia. He was the son of the river god and a nymph. He was extremely handsome. Nemesis lured him to the edge of a lake where Narcissus was so engrossed in admiring his reflection that he ended up drowning. In today's world, narcissism is a theory used in psychoanalysis; the theories have the beginnings in the book on narcissism by Sigmund Freud. Additionally, the American Psychiatrist association classifies narcissism as a mental disorder.

Narcissism is a personality trait disorder. Most

psychologist and psychoanalysis experts all agree that narcissism is a cultural and social problem that is increasing on a daily basis. There is healthy narcissism; most psychologists refer to this as a show of healthy self-love. However, most psychoanalysts agree that the line between healthy self-love and narcissistic tendencies is very narrow, and healthy self-love can easily escalate into narcissism without a person's knowledge. Obsession over one's own physical appearance at unnatural levels can lead to be a distraction from the person's daily life and activities.

In fact, narcissism personality disorder is one of the three dark personalities or the ***dark triad*** together with Machiavellianism, and Psychopathy. The dark triad is coined die to the fact that these three disorders are all considered to have malevolent qualities.

However, you should not confuse narcissism with egocentrism. Surely, the narcissists are filled to the brim with ego just like the egocentrics, but there is still a difference. The narcissists get their fix of admiration or whatever supply it is that they need for the moment when it comes from someone else.

Dealing with narcissism is very difficult, especially because the people suffering from it do not think of it as a problem. In fact, the people who suffer from narcissism thinks they are perfectly fine and normal. In case there is anything or anyone that forces them to double check the way they live their lives, they will do their best to cover the actual facts that appears to them as ***attacks*** and live on.

Also, don't you ever try to insist or even point out the problem to them or you are in for a big and maybe even bloody fight.

In this book, we shall look at some of the ways by which one can get over narcissism or deal with a narcissistic behavior.

Chapter 1: Understanding Narcissism

A narcissist is a person who has a personality disorder in which he or she is excessively preoccupied with dominance, power, prestige, and vanity. They do not realize the destruction they cause to themselves and others. A so-called narcissist can do things without noticing the feelings of the people around them. They consider themselves truly superior and they need to be respected. You can call them vain or selfish, those are just some of the common labels used by many towards narcissists. They are involved in feelings, as for them it's only normal to feel hurt. They came up with this *narcissist* version of themselves so that it can serve as the shock absorber.

However, a narcissistic pain is different from other types of emotional pain. People who suffer from narcissism often display attitudes like being snobbish, patronizing or even disdain. For example, he or she may complain about a bartender's rudeness or stupidity or conclude a medical evaluation with a condescending evaluation of the physician.

A personality disorder is a kind of pattern and behavior that deviates from the norm individual's culture. This pattern is seen in the following areas: cognition; interpersonal functioning; impulse control; or affect. The enduring pattern is not exactly flexible and it can also be seen at one's early childhood characteristics. The pattern is stable and is in long duration.

Narcissism is more prevalent in males than females. However, as time passed by and when they suppress all the feelings, this disorder is to decreased and symptoms become lesser at the age of the 40s to 50s. There are things that cause a person to become a narcissist. Researchers today don't exactly know what causes a person to eventually turn into a narcissist. There are many theories, however, only about the possible cause of narcissistic personality disorder.

Most professionals subscribe to a bio-psychosocial model of causation – that is, the cause of are likely due to biological and genetic factors, social factors, such as how people react to one another starting from their early age up to the present. Consider the psychological factors, which are the personality and temperaments of a human being shaped by the environment and the learned coping skills to deal with stress. This suggests that there is no single factor responsible in becoming a narcissist – rather, it is the complex and likely intertwined nature of all factors that are important. If a person has this personality disorder, they are suggested to become a carrier of it and pass it down to their unknowing children.

There are actually treatments of this personality disorder, which typically involves long-term psycho treatment or psychotherapy, with a therapist who has a wide experience in treating this kind of personality disorder. Some medications can actually help with specific sets of symptoms. The person with this kind of disorder usually exaggerate things around him, they also tend to have a daydreaming about fantasies of beauty, success and power over dominating their thoughts. This type of person is also too sensitive. They need to be admired in everything they do at all times. If not, they will be hurt deep inside.

They also tend to manipulate and take advantage of the people around them using their emotional feelings that people around them needs to consider, as a weapon. They lack empathy that makes us feel and recognize the feelings of needs of others. These types of people also are the envy type ones and their behavior appears to us as haughty or arrogant.

A person with untreated Narcissistic Personality Disorder has a higher chance of substance abuse including drugs and alcohol, depression, problems with a relationship, difficulties at work or school and suicidal behaviors or thoughts. Recent studies found out that males with narcissism have higher measures of *cortisol* in their blood. *Cortisol* is a stress hormone, so basically this disorder is caused by too much stress triggered by experience from childhood up to the point where they cannot handle it anymore.

Even those who do not have so much stress have higher levels of *cortisol*. High levels of *cortisol* is linked to a greater risk of developing some kind of heart problems. Family members of somebody with this disorder describe the sufferer as controlling and forever dissatisfied with what anybody around them does. The narcissist will never fail blame others and make them feel guilty of their problems and what they are into now. They are described as short and ill tempered. They lose their tempers at the slightest provocation and think that every little thing is not going their way. They will think that people around them always turns their backs and gives them a silent treatment.

Worst cases can turn a human being to someone who is

very abusive both physically and sexually. Living with a narcissist can feel as if you're living a very confusing nightmare. It's like you are getting into jail with a no exact way of escape. The spouse, co-workers, boss, and even the parent can sometimes get stuck in a relationship they find very hard to escape from. The emotional and the physical damages caused by somebody with the disorder can be severe. Health care professionals aren't an exception to emotional exhaustion.

Narcissists strive to defend their fragile self-esteem through the use of facade and carefully produced blind spots in their thinking. Living in a fantasy world, where they meet all their needs and unrealistic expectations take the place of life. They feel superior with this wonderland that they made up in their heads without noticing the effects they are making to the people around them. They become involved in beauty, material things, and shallowly develop interest in things that are not real such as soap operas, movies, games, and rock stars.

They fear their feelings. They cannot gain and keep a deep friendship or intimacy and cannot develop a mature love relationship. A fantasy world can be a sweet escape for a narcissist and can also become an attempt not to see what is really there in order to build up self-esteem. Narcissist people process information, emotions, and unresolved pain to make up for their hidden damaged childhood. They love achieving something with their own imaginations in their created world and they often place an unrealistic demand to someone else just to feel better. They are not one to tolerate negative emotional distress, as they are not very good at it. They usually push it to others and blame them instead of looking closer to see their own part of the problem. This is the defense of projection – when a certain person does not like him or herself, they get angry to those who have some of the likable traits.

The Self-image is distorted in narcissistic point of view and the person believes that he is more superior than others. An over the top self-esteem is a defense to cover up the unforgettable shame deep within. Grandiosity is an insidious error in thinking that it is a prevention and it stops them from blaming themselves and becoming depressed or disintegrated.

Narcissist people like to hear the sound of their own voice. They are individuals that thrive on being the center of attraction and attention who tends to put down others whom they feel is inferior. At work, a narcissist is power hungry and will go to great lengths to gain power. Learning if you are with a narcissist can be quite difficult and confusing in the sense that you also might be confused about what you feel towards the narcissist you are with.

Narcissists prefer to work under their own set of rules. Narcissist only cares about themselves and therefore, when working with a narcissist, always remember that they will never be a great buddy to be with. They will befriend you to convert you into one of their victims or supply sources, will do favors expecting a big return and you will do the same thing as well to them. Unfortunately, in the workplace you can't just do anything that you want to this person and walk away without so much as an issue. So the best thing to do is to go along with him or her. Getting in touch with a narcissist more often will keep them from thinking you don't like them. But be careful of getting too close with a narcissist because they think different and digest words from you differently. Narcissist do expect you to be immediately responsive the moment they demand attention just like a normal boss in your company who wants you to immediately follow him in everything he demands.

Sharing your emotions to a narcissist is a big no because you are forcing them to prioritize your feelings. The next best thing that you can actually do is focus on solutions and not the problem. Narcissist likes to focus on the problem and turn it over, around, rearrange, and practically dissect it to pieces. They tend to make things very complicated. Stop looking at the glass as if it is half empty. The best thing that you can do is flip it and influence the narcissist to see the other side of truth.

It's actually a good choice to just present several solutions. Narcissist likes to be in control and they'd love you if you have this much-favored ability to offer them options. This is one of the several ways that you can make them feel as if you truly respect their opinion and that you are asking them to take control and show you what they are made of. If it still does not work out, you best last option is to make them feel good about themselves, unique, and special. Narcissists wants to be praised and they like the feeling that they are higher than you. They get high off of being in power and they thrive in attention and admiration. If you want them to be happily productive for you, simply let them know how great they are. Praising them makes them feel at peace.

When a narcissist grows up, they harbor the irrational belief that the person they choose as a partner will give them perfect love and make up for all hurts and slights of their life. This burning desire for getting unconditional love is an unresolved need from their damaged childhood. While most adults find the good thing about unconditional, understand also that it rarely happens. This is because the people we love usually holding us somehow responsible for our actions. Think carefully about imposing your neediness and bad behavior towards others.

Being a narcissist is not an easy thing, people with this kind of disorder don't need to be rejected and taken for granted. They believe that everything is fine because that's the way they grew up with, which is a normal thing for them. People with this kind of disorder need more attention and understanding, no one wishes to be born with this disorder. People with a narcissistic behavior have a sense of entitlement that allows them to break the rules of society. They believe that laws do not apply to them and they do not feel remorse when they get caught. However, they are upset over any inconveniences they suffer as a result of being busted. They believe they have the right to do whatever it takes to get short term gratification without suffering any consequences.

Narcissism in Everyday Life

We have already defined narcissism, but how does it relate to normal everyday life? To have a better understanding of narcissism, let us look at a fictional character Tom.

Tom is a regional cooperate manager. At first glance, he is a gem. He seems pleasant, charming, and endearing; all the traits you would expect from someone in his position. However, the moment you get to know Tom more, you start to realize some things that may not necessarily seem charming. Tom hates it when you contradict him in meetings, either at work or social settings. He is not as open to suggestion as you might believe. He thinks his opinions are of utmost importance, and for this reason, he expresses them freely without any consideration for anyone else. He may ask for your opinions but at this stage it is only a formality and not something he would devote his attention to. He hates challenges, he is unsure of winning, and loathes criticism. He acts as if he is a demigod who deserves worship. He wants his words to be considered regarded as the Gospel and there is no argument beyond that. If he is kept waiting, or things do not go according to what he deems to be the correct way, in this case his way, he can blow things out of proportion. Throwing tantrums or delving into an extremely unpleasant behavior is easy for such a person. He will hold grudges against people who stand up to him, regardless of whether they were right or not. This behavior is downright childish and is also not the only childish behavior he will exhibit. As a man who is used to getting his way, at restaurants, he is the person who must get the table he wants at the snap of a finger. When he does not get the table, or the service he wants, he is quick to throw an anger fit. For these reasons, Tom has no real friends. His self-inflated ego and sense of importance gradually throw him out of favor of almost all his acquaintances. Although he has a downright charming persona and a general gentlemanly attitude, all of it falls apart slowly as you get to know him more. Everyone who gets to know him eventually gets tired of him and his godlike, self-centered attitude. Due to his self-centeredness, he has difficulty connecting with people, as well as being sensitive to their needs or wants. Do not get me wrong, Tom helps a few people, but only when it casts him in a positive light or advances his own personal agenda. It is also debatable that Tom does not consider himself friends with anybody. As far as he is concerned, he owes a few people a few favors. He sees people as resources rather than friends. He uses them to get his will done.

For Tom, there is no separation from his self-righteousness. For this reason, his wife, children, and neighbors find it difficult to communicate with him as well as live with him because he expects everybody to agree with his opinions. Tom is a narcissist through and through. And getting him to admit this will prove to be an uphill task. I am not saying Tom is a bad person. He might have a misplaced sense of self-righteousness that may seem absolutely right to him but is heavily flawed from another perspective. He may never realize this because the only perspective he is willing to consider is his own. If his wife is not a quiet woman, he is extremely likely to end up quarrelling with her often for petty reasons. A family life for such a person may be harder to maintain than for normal people. As a parent, his communication with the kids will be heavily one sided.

As I have said, narcissism, to some degree, is healthy. Confidence and solid faith in one's abilities is sometimes misinterpreted as narcissism. Confidence or over confidence can sometimes be considered arrogance but it is almost never a narcissistic trait. There are many confident people in the world; people who believe in themselves and their abilities. Absolute faith in one's abilities cannot be summarized as narcissism. The only difference between these people and a pathological narcissist is that unlike the narcissist, they do not consider themselves a cut above the rest (better than anyone) or demand that they be accorded special treatment. They do not insist that they stand above their peers and deserve special treatment. They are more devoted to the job or the task at hand. A confident and strong-willed individual is more likely to be successful than a narcissist. While a narcissist doles away admiring himself the confident person gets the job done.

This is not to mean that they do not consider themselves the best in their field of study; no, they simply are not envious or harbor any grudge against other accomplished people in the same field of study as them.

They are aware of their needs and feelings as well as those of people around them. They do not think that every opportunity to help someone else is an opportunity to advance their own agenda. They genuinely care about others. The narcissistic individual on the other hand is the opposite. He looks for loopholes and ways to divert every opportunity in his favor regardless of its impact on the people around him. Jealousy and peer rivalry might also induce him to drag down the people he envies. A narcissist may even go so far as to refuse helping a colleague who works in the same field of study that he does. All out of hatred for that person!

Here are some of the main characteristics a pathological narcissist will display.

1. They always feel entitled, as if everything is their right.
2. They are constant attention-seekers who desire admiration most times.

3. They are exploitive. They will take advantage of a child if it will advance their self-centered agenda.
4. If your suffering or distress will not advance his or her agenda, then it is of little concern to them. They are unable to identify with any feeling or emotion that is not helpful to the attainment of their agenda.
5. Jealousy is their middle name. When someone else gets the prize instead of him or her, he or she will be envious and feel like it should have been him or her.
6. They are extremely arrogant.
7. They are preoccupied with dreams of grandeur, unlimited success, beauty, ideal love, and marriage. They believe that their brilliance is comparable to Albert Einstein's.

Chapter 2: 10 Common Myths About Narcissism

We basically have an idea what narcissism is, however, not everything that we know about it is true. Just like any other illness or condition, there would be a bunch of people who would tell you what to do or what not to do whenever around *this* person, or what habits or mannerisms will tell you that *this* certain person is suffering from the sickness or disorder being currently talked about.

It is good that we know how to identify the *possible* signs from someone who is suffering from narcissism, but not who frequently does the *possible* signs are already narcissist. The problem with people is that whenever they do not know anything, they *try* to appear like they know it by piecing together a couple of signs, mannerisms, or attitude of a certain person and assume tons of things from there.

You have to understand that not everything that we hear from our elders, those who have experienced first hand a certain length of time with a narcissist, or have a narcissist for a family member are true and can be found in all narcissists. Your assumptions and the assumptions on the narcissism of people around you aren't always right, as well. Is it making you confused? Let us proceed.

1. All narcissist have low self-esteem and are always insecure.

While looking at a list of the attitudes and behavior of a narcissist, you can almost agree to this myth without any hint of difficulty. It is not the case, however. Contrary to this popular belief, a narcissist does not adore themselves just because they are trying to protect their image, or they are badly wounded inside that they are trying to look very, very fine.

In fact, they do not need to defend themselves because, in truth, narcissist thinks they are the best at everything. If you're the best at everything what is the point of being insecure or even have low self-esteem? See, that is how serious narcissists are about adoring themselves.

They do not adore themselves for protection or just to cope. They adore themselves because they think they are a *supreme being*. It is that simple, no need for you to further understand why they do this and that. There is no use telling these people or suggesting having someone help them increase their self-esteem. The problem is, their self-esteem has already skyrocketed and seems like it won't be back even after a century.

2. Narcissism = Physical Vanity

Not really. Yes, narcissism is strongly connected to physical vanity, but it is not the only thing that makes these people live and breathe. Just because a person has the addiction or unbearable habit of looking in the mirror does not exactly mean they are already narcissistic.

One ***self-obsessive*** habit alone does not make a narcissistic. A narcissist's choice, wherever you look whether it is inside or out, will always be his or herself. They will simply choose themselves over anything and anyone and this choice will be made without even a sweat or a twitch of the eyebrows from the difficulty of the decision.

There are so many things that complete a narcissistic like entitlement, antisocial behavior, relationship problems, materialism, and more. This disorder is more than skin deep, it is way beyond to the point of being unreasonably self-obsessed.

3. Deep down, they have a reason for being the narcissist that they are.

This is not true. Narcissists just love themselves like

that. In fact, the term love itself is wrong to be used on them as the *love* that they practice or use on themselves is love ***that is not for their real selves***.

Narcissists are like drunken people inside a bar who think they already love the person who is dancing in the dark right in front of them. However, as soon as they sober up or the light is shed on the face of the person they are facing, they realize that it was just a night that went uncontrollably fun and they lost control. They simply wake up realizing that there never has been that sort of *love* that bloomed the night before.

The good thing about the drunken party-goers is that they still get to wake up from this dream. Such is not the case with narcissist people. This is the problem, they cannot wake up from this *drunken sort of love* and annoyingly so, we simply have to endure their company or ignore them altogether.

There is simply no reason behind their narcissism. They

simply think of themselves like *Gods* or *legends* and if you take the time to test their intelligence and beauty, almost always, they are average.

4. Narcissists do not have an idea that they are narcissists

When it comes to personality disorders, we usually have this notion that the sufferer of the disorder usually do not know that he is actually suffering from it. While this may apply to some like the multiple personality disorder this is not the case with narcissism.

Some narcissistic people cannot exactly pinpoint what is going on with them or if there is a disorder that they are suffering from. Yes, there are some who know exactly that they are narcissistic and would even think about it thoroughly. However, if there is one thing that all of them surely know, it is the fact that *they lack something that every other human have* and this *lacking* is something that they can use to their full advantage.

That missing part is, yes, empathy. They know this and they also know that this is should be a secret, a very deep and dark one that nobody else should ever know.

Now, comes *denial* in the picture and you should know that this comes hand-in-hand in being a narcissist. Every narcissist knows what they lack and they will not hesitate to go all out just to deny it.

5. Narcissism equates to high self-esteem

When the word narcissism is mentioned to us, we usually and unconsciously correlate it with a skyrocketing self-esteem. This is not true as one can have a very high self-esteem, but they are not necessarily narcissistic.

People with self-esteem, even those who have a skyrocketing one are still capable of having and maintaining a healthy relationship. That is exactly what our narcissistic ones are not capable of. Yes, they care about what you can do for them, but as soon as they have realized that you are of no use, you are officially out of the picture in a snap.

Do not expect for even a drop of sweat coming out of a narcissist as they make this decision of burning bridges because they are like the master switch that really turns everything off as soon as you flip it. There is simply no feeling, whatsoever. For them, relationships are nothing but pure business for them and they do not care even somebody else gets hurt as long as that somebody isn't them.

5. Being narcissistic is necessary for success

Just because you see Donald Trump's face gracing your television screen from time to time, it does not mean that narcissism is necessary for one to be successful. Yes, he is undeniably successful, but narcissism nor high self-esteem isn't the key to success. A very high self-esteem or narcissism, for that matter, is not correlated with success as there are different kinds of people who are very successful.

While it is true that to be successful one needs to be bold and daring, some of the traits that are very strong, high self-esteem cannot be treated as a trait that is a necessity for success. If a person has very high self-esteem but does not have the persistence, discipline, and creativity, success will most likely stay as a mere objective and nothing more.

6. Narcissism can be beneficial

Once you get to partially understand how narcissism works, you might get to the conclusion that it actually is somehow beneficial to the narcissist himself. You might even get to the point where you think that narcissism can be healthy.

I am sorry that I'd have to burst your bubble here, but what you are thinking is very, very wrong. While narcissism can appear as if it is helping the person who is actually suffering from it, it is but a false outcome. Whatever sort of success or benefit the narcissist is experiencing, they are merely short-term success.

Here, let me paint you a little picture to make things clearer for you.

Imagine the narcissist as a relatively small roller coaster car on a small roller coaster. A small roller coaster would mean small dips, short thrills, and short tracks.

The narcissist thinks otherwise. Everything that your naked eye can see and your normal brain can process about the small roller coaster car will be the exact opposite for the narcissist.

The narcissist thinks that he or she, being the roller coaster car, is big and gets to travel on a long, high, and big track. Actually, that's an understatement. They'd most likely think they are humongous and perfect. They would think they are incomparable not only in terms of size and quality but also in every thing. Yes, for them, they have it all absolutely covered.

Once the roller coaster starts running, you, being the rider, would enjoy it for a bit. However, since you know that it is small, you know that this enjoyment would not last and that you will be back on the ground, standing on your feet, in no time.

Our dear narcissist wouldn't care about what you think, of course. They are humongous and perfect! What have you to say, little rider, that is of any value? Your opinion and what you know does not matter to them, at all!

And so, your roller coaster ride ended without even a bang, you get off the car and walk back home. Dull and average, right? The narcissist doesn't care about that. He will never realize what you saw because he is too blinded by his made up image to even bother stepping back to look at the big picture.

The roller coaster has its loops, but since it is small, high will soon become low. The roller coaster car, being the narcissist itself, would never realize that he or she has come back down and that the whole ride has already stopped. They'd be stuck in their imaginary glory of an endless roller coaster ride where the car never goes back down.

7. Narcissists love themselves to death and beyond

Narcissists adore themselves in whatever angle they look at the mirror and in whatever nook and cranny they search through their inner selves. This is evident in just about every narcissist. There is this expression often used in movies by a narcissist character: *"I love myself."*

However, you have to realize that what we mostly see from a narcissist is merely a fraction of the truth. What we see and think about a narcissist is merely what the ***inner narcissist or the mastermind*** wants us to see.

Mastermind? Yes, there is one living in the very

depths of every narcissist's persona. I will tell you all about it in the next chapter.

Going back to our topic that is our usual perception about narcissists who love themselves to hell and back, well, it is simply not true. Narcissists are completely not capable of caring for someone and when it comes to loving themselves, they are *completely* incapable of this as well.

You must be thinking right now how absorbed they are of themselves that you do not get how they are incapable of self-love.

Let me explain it to you, then. You have to understand first that narcissists do not love themselves. Whatever it is that you see from narcissists that portray self-love to you, in reality, can be anything, but self-love.

What you see is merely a display of what we may call a compulsive obsession to the ***made-up*** version of themselves. If you think there are some people in your school or office that you can easily tag as fake, they are nothing compared to narcissists.

Narcissists are the real fake sorts of people. When we look at narcissists, what we actually see on the surface is a solidified and fortified persona made up of layers and layers of self-projection that they had amassed for so many years. Self-projection is their craft and they have perfected it to the point of them believing their own lies. This dedication to self-project a *goody-two-shoes* image is what makes us think that they are so in love with their selves.

8. All narcissists are, pretty much, the same

This is, yet, another misconception as not all narcissists are the same. While they all share that some traits like the complete lack of empathy or pathological lying, there are still different kinds of narcissists. There are some who are openly narcissistic, some who try their best to hide it but wanted to stick out in a subtle and sneaky way, there are also some who are obsessed with their physical looks, and more.

9. Narcissists are very prone to suicide

Suicide is *usually* a big **NO** for narcissists. It is true that some narcissists resort to suicide, but that would be a rare case, Suicide is simply an exact opposite of the idea of narcissism. This myth is, again, another product of confusion from various personality disorders.

Yes, other types of personality disorders are very much prone to suicide, but if it is narcissism we are talking about, expect them to either run for help or do it themselves in a crazy manner.

Why don't we try putting ourselves in the shoes of a narcissistic and think like them? In the first place, if you *think* that *you really love yourself that much,* why get rid of the world of yet another blessing by killing yourself? That would be depriving the rest of the world of the greatness that you, as a narcissist, can impart!

Usually, if a narcissist encounters a challenging phase in

life or crisis, he will try to overcome it and there are many ways for him to do it without resorting to suicide. Most of a narcissist's choices are therapy sessions or get strangely creative and make their own drama.

You see, whenever we, normal or narcissist, encounter a life crisis we always come out of it wounded. Normal people would usually nurse themselves or find someone who can help them nurse their wounds so they can get back on track and move on with their lives. Narcissists, on the other hand, won't burden themselves in nursing their wounds. What they would do is look for someone else to suck energy from and use the said energy so their wounds can heal quickly and they would feel better.

These methods are a narcissist's shortcut to getting over it or getting better. When a narcissist refers himself for therapy, this is so they can suck dry the energy of people involved in the therapy or the therapist himself. Some narcissists, instead of involving themselves in therapy, prefer to create some sort of drama like feigning illness, pull a crazy life stunt, commit a crime, lie, or basically do anything that will get them that badly needed ***energy*** so he can heal quickly.

10. Narcissism is curable by medication and therapy

While other personality disorder, such as borderline personality disorder, can be treated with therapy and other methods, narcissism is a different story.

When a person is suffering from narcissism, what they lack is empathy, the proper judgment of what is wrong or right, and many other traits. Medication nor therapy simply cannot recreate and instill the needed *normal traits* to a narcissist, thus it is impossible to treat this disorder.

Another thing that a narcissist's relative or loved one should take note of is bringing the narcissist to a therapist. This would be a big mistake as you will not only spend money without getting the proper result from the treatment, you will also help your relative supply his or her narcissism in a not-so-good way.

Chapter 3: A Narcissist's True Self And False Self

Before we move on to recognizing the signs and symptoms or some other details regarding narcissism, we have to start from the root of it all. It is essential for you to know the importance of the true and false selves to help you understand narcissism better.

Specialists and other medical practitioners use the terms ***true self*** and ***false self*** when studying or talking about narcissism.

When someone says *mastermind,* what usually comes into mind is the image of a big, bad boss of a syndicate who formulates and refines the plans before they carry out a crime. One can imagine how crafty, ruthless, sadistic, and deceitful a mastermind is. A narcissist's true self is utterly clever and crafty, thus it is only fitting to call it the mastermind. That is how you can easily picture a narcissist's *true self.*

The True Self

So, what is the *true self,* what does it do, and what is its role in narcissism?

It all starts when one is born. That innocent little baby, who is new to the concept of the world and the people around him or her, is the true self.

Most of the true selves, as they grow up, had to learn to fight life's battles by growing, toughening up, and learning life's lessons to survive. The true self has to go through life's long path to success and contentment.

Life's long path is introduced to us by our parents or elders little by little as we age and we are taught how to fight life's battles by looking at it in the face, right in the eye. Ideas, inspirations, and knowledge are passed to us in order for us to survive this life-long fight and come out triumphant.

And so, as we grow up, we become busy in adapting all these teachings coming from our elders and applying them to our own lives in order to survive. Also, normally, a *real self* has the innate ability to empathize. The *real self* observes and respects coexistence. It practices the ability to live and let live as much as it can without having to sacrifice himself or others.

That is the usual and normal case where ***real selves*** are busy preparing and learning how to fight fairly and squarely as they spend their years on the face of the earth. Surely a difficult path, but that is how life goes for everyone, right?

Not exactly. There are some unlucky ones whose childhood phase gets all messed up either by experiences like something traumatic, tragic, unfair treatment, and more. When narcissism starts from childhood, the root cause is usually something very deep that the young mind cannot grasp, no matter how many times it attempts to take control of what is going on.

This is where the real self's point of view gets too distracted because of the strong desire to cope and move on with life. However, it comes to a crucial point where the real self becomes trapped, helpless, and threatened.

In this phase, there are a couple of defense mechanisms that a trapped *real self* can come up with in order to escape the very difficult situation. These defense mechanisms can range anywhere from a wide array of mental disorders like ADHD, panic, anxiety, depression, post-traumatic stress, schizophrenia, compulsive obsession, bipolar, and more.

There are also the various personality disorders that the brain may use as a defense mechanism. It can be borderline personality disorder, paranoia, multiple personality, narcissism or some other personality disorder. Worse case scenario is when the real self cannot come up with any of these mental or personality disorders to use as its ultimate defense and just resorts to end everything through suicide.

These wide array of defense mechanisms cannot be chosen by the conscious or real self. Whatever sort of defense mechanism comes out of a person is chosen by the subconscious alone. There is no way that one can control and tell the subconscious what to choose for its defense mechanism.

The False Self

The false self is the carefully crafted, nurtured, and fortified version of the *true self*. False selves aren't instantly made. It takes a narcissist a couple of decades to polish and teach the false self the act of smooth deception. The deception has to be smooth enough that even the narcissist himself already believes the lies that the false self is spreading.

For a narcissist, this is the point in life where his ***false self*** is born. The event in life, where the subconscious goes on autopilot and takes over to choose a defense mechanism or escape, has to be triggered. One can never plan or even tell when the subconscious will take over because it serves as your entire persona's plan B or emergency kit.

A narcissist's *true self,* after a traumatizing experience, is always badly wounded. The trigger occurs when the brain cannot handle what is currently happening anymore. It may be due to too much pain or a cocktail of strong emotions that the individual is currently exposed to. When things like this happen and the brain cannot process it anymore, its response is to shut down.

That's the *real self* signing out to make itself a tiny, yet secured little fortress in the deepest part of the brain where no one can bother it anymore. The body will end up like a car without its driver, merely an empty vessel. Once this takes place, the subconscious kicks in and runs in autopilot mode in an attempt to save the true self. The subconscious comes up on its own a *defense mechanism* that doubles as an *escape*

The result is the tangible, annoying, unreasonable, abusive, seemingly self-absorbed, usually intolerable machine called the ***false self.***

Think of the narcissist as a snail. The true self is the soft and squishy snail while the false self is the shell. Whenever something bad is bound to happen, the snail hides itself under the shell for protection. That is how true and false self work with each other. It is a facade, just like a mask that knows very well how to hide a secret.

One can nurture the false self or make it repair itself by smothering it with affirmations.

There is yet another problem with the narcissist. Yes, the true self created the false self, but as the false self is being nurtured and gets to refine its craft of deception as the days and years go by, it starts to take over the whole person.

This causes the real self to become weak and get buried into the depths of the person. The real self also becomes confused about ***who he or she really is*** because of the smooth deception that the false self practices. As the disorder progresses, the narcissist's view about the separation of real and false self becomes too blurry that it doesn't recognize anymore which is which. This lack of sense of self becomes the lifetime burden of a narcissist, without him even realizing what has become of him.

Why Does the Damaged Real Self Need the False Self?

Simple, because the damaged real self needs a

protection and it sees the false self as very capable of that role.

The real self becomes too damaged and traumatized that it completely forgets its capability to heal and become stronger through time. This leads the real self to think that it will need the false self for life and that is exactly what it does: rely on the false self for a lifetime.

In turn, the false self, while it annoys the heck out of the people around it and may even cause them harm, makes the real self feel secured for a lifetime. This is due to the false self's display of everything that the real self is not. It is a facade that is very tough to crack, it serves as a proxy for the real self and has the ability to absorb almost any amount of pain the real self cannot take. It takes care of the negative emotions or hurt and makes sure that it doesn't reach the real self's sanctuary. It is the real self's protective cloak that gives the assurance that it will never let the real self experience the pain that it went through or any kind of pain anymore.

What Makes the False Selves So Bad?

The whole idea of the false self may sound to you like a hopeless romantic stuck in a tragic love story. It sounds sweet, but the false self is a double-sided blade. It may give the real self a very secure sanctuary, but it also leads the real self to a silent self-destruction.

How so? They are always in denial and they are willing to do just about anything in order to keep their facade smooth and perfect.

Normally, when a person picks a romantic partner, they keep themselves in each other's companies and strive to improve each other. Now, when a normal person has a narcissist for a romantic partner, the beginning of the relationship may be balloons, ice creams, bike rides, the sunshine, and everything sweet. However, as the relationship matures, the normal partner will start noticing the self-importance or abuse that the narcissist partner does.

A narcissist partner, at first, will show you all the best that he is and the good things he can do. For him, you are a new supply source, a new victim. You and your narcissist partner will be able to stay smoothly together as long as you can adjust and keep up with his facade. This means you have to put up with almost everything about your relationship being unfair and everything should be in his favor.

However, if you start criticizing your narcissist partner's ways or you want to make him compromise with you, he will start seeing you as an attack or someone who wants to inflict pain to the real self. To a normal person, this will lead him to inspect and take a closer look at himself and try to work it out with his partner.

To a narcissist, this may also lead him to a closer inspection of himself and he knows that this will destroy the facade he has built for so many years. In this kind of event, a narcissist may become aggressive towards you because he is doing his best to protect the facade even if it means hurting you. He doesn't care anyway, as long as he doesn't get hurt.

There is no way that you can get rid of a narcissist's facade, as he will surely protect it with his life. He will always be in denial of whatever it is that you say is wrong about him and denying is very easy for him as he also believes in his carefully woven lies. He is unable to recognize the truth from the lies anymore and trying to shove the fact down his throat will not do you any good.

Also, narcissists as we have witnessed for so many years, are almost always one of the well-achieved, rich, and famous people. This is because being applauded, treated as a VIP, and given too much attention is far too irresistible for them. These kind of treatments feed their being narcissists and if it means to strive hard to get up there will give them their much-needed attention, there's no more hesitating for them. They will do whatever it takes just to get there and once they are up there, they will surely bask in the glory.

A Narcissist's Supply Source

The term *supply source* will be repeated in this book several times. You may already have a bit of an idea once you come across these words, however, give me the honor of explaining them further to you and point out the roles of a supply source in a narcissist's life.

What is A Supply Source?

A supply source is a person or a group of people that satisfies the self-absorbed cravings of a narcissist. You can compare it to the game Pac-Man. Imagine the narcissist as Pac-Man and the ghosts as the supply source.

The narcissist doesn't put any boundaries between him and the supply source, meaning if the narcissist wants to devour the energies of the supply source, deplete it or abuse it just to satisfy his narcissistic needs, he will do so without even caring about what happens to the supply source afterwards.

After all, the supply source is nothing but a source for the narcissist and he would not even bother finding out if the supply source has the ability to feel or not. For the narcissist, the supply source is a part of him as long as the supply source is able to provide him everything that he needs. He also has certain expectations that the supply source *should* be able to live up to. If not, the narcissist finds a new supply source that is willing enough or is very capable to provide him what he needs.

Types of Narcissistic Supply Source

There are two types of the narcissistic supply source and they are the *primary and secondary* sources.

The primary source of narcissistic supply is a person or a group of people who gives the narcissist his fix of narcissistic supply on a random basis.

The secondary source of narcissistic supply is a person or group of people that satisfies the narcissist's needs on a daily, or consistent basis. This group includes the family members of the narcissist, partner, colleagues, classmates, teachers or professors, friends, and anyone else that shares a relationship with the narcissist.

What are the Narcissistic Supplies?

Approval

Admiration

Applause

Compliments

Money

Sexual Dominance

Adulation

Affirmation

Celebrity Status and VIP Treatment

Attention

Intimidation

Respect

Yes, the narcissists think they are ***that*** entitled to deserve all those listed above. These supplies should come to the narcissist in a steady stream and they will make sure that it does. They are willing to go through great lengths just to see to it that their needs and cravings are satisfied.

To a narcissist, a little disturbance to that steady stream of supplies means it is already time for him to start looking for a new supply source and ditch the non-cooperating, old, and depleted source.

Since we have two types of the narcissistic supply source that very well means that we also have two types of narcissistic supplies.

The primary narcissistic supply is any form of attention, be it public, interpersonal, or public. The narcissist does not care if the attention given to them is negative or positive. To them, attention is attention, no matter what and if it means he should keep the notorious image because he gets a steady stream of supply from it, he will. He does not care about the substance as long as he has his audience and their perception of his greatness.

The secondary narcissistic supply, on the other hand, is made up of the needs of the narcissist to have a normal life, a partner, and the ability to provide for himself with more than what he really needs. To this, the narcissist will insist on living a normal life, function and appear normal. If it doesn't seem to him that he is living a normal life, the fact that his life looks normal to other people will do.

Why do Narcissist Resort to Supplies and Sources?

A narcissist, generally, has no sense of self. That leads to the absence of the *sense of self-worth.* Take note, the sense of self and self-worth is innate and built-in to us.

As soon as a person loses his grasp on his *real self,* with it comes the sense of self and self-worth. That is all three very essential things to human survival saying goodbye to you as they hide in the deepest places of your brain. And then you turn into a narcissist.

This *loss* makes the narcissist turn to other people to satisfy their need to feel good about themselves. We all have the need to feel good about ourselves and this is normal as long as it is kept in moderation. The narcissist, on the other hand, has nothing normal going on with his need about feeling good about himself because he is insatiable. His need to re-affirm his greatness has become distorted and it is comparable to a drug addict who doesn't care about the drug's dosage anymore. The only thing that matters to the narcissist is his satisfaction.

Emotions and Narcissism, Is it Possible?

Just because a narcissist lacks empathy, it does not necessarily mean that he does not have any kind of emotion. Still, consider the fact that a narcissist is still a human being, gifted with a wide array of emotions, both negative and positive.

While it is true that a narcissist is very skillful in hiding or repressing his or her emotions, one should know that this is just a fraction of the narcissist's whole persona. Also remember, in order for someone to be able to hide something, he ***has to have it.***

So, where exactly does a narcissist hide his or her emotions?

Remember how a narcissist's false self is born? When a false self is born, the real self should vacate the body in order for the false self to have a space where he or she can live and grow.

As the false self emerges on the surface of the real self's body, the real self becomes busy packing almost everything that has something to do with the old him that reminds the real self about who he or she really is.

This packing event usually includes the emotions, mannerisms, and dominant behavior that the real self has. After that, the real self and its pack hides itself in the deepest and farthest corner of the brain where it can live in peace.

Packing and hiding are very easy to do that the real self can do it as soon as the brain shuts down due to too much emotion. The problem is, once the real self and everything that has something to do with it is packed and hidden away neatly, relocating the whole package and unpacking it becomes a feat.

This is due to the false self's smooth lies and occupation of the body that the real self owned and previously occupied. Relocating and unpacking the real self's package without bothering or even upsetting the false self is impossible. Add to that the fact that the real self, who has become very comfortable and in peace in its secret sanctuary, is now afraid to feel anything and everything that it used to feel before, including the good emotions.

With all these knots and confusions, the real self to avoid more conflicts opts to just repress the emotions that might come out. The real self does its best repressing all of it because it knows what will happen. It knows that if it tries to find one end of the knot and try to fix everything from there, another more confusing and deeper problem will just arise.

A Narcissist's Trick

Understand that the narcissist have an idea of what is really happening with him. Some may be able to point out that narcissism is the issue while some may not. Yes, the narcissist can still feel, but compared to our full-color, 3D emotions, a narcissist only gets a monochrome and very blurry, splotchy image.

This leads narcissists into thinking that other people are ridiculous for having too many emotions. They simply do not understand why and how we feel way too much compared to them. Narcissists tend to react in a very aggressive manner, get embarrassed, suspicious, and even dumbfounded whenever confronted by a very emotional experience with other people. Why? Because these raw emotions coming from normal people that surround them reminds them how weak and vulnerable their real selves are.

What they do in order to avoid this kind of situation is fake it. Since narcissists do not understand where full-blown emotions come from, why and how it exists, they tend to think that we, normal people, are just faking it because we want to achieve something.

This leads them to think that faking it all together is perfectly fine since they also need to achieve something. Also, even if it is not exactly okay with us, they do not care anyway. What matters to them is that they get to act it out so they can blend in with us.

Narcissists emulate and simulate our emotions mostly through practicing and perfecting the craft of mimicking our expressions. You can compare this emulation and simulation to a child.

Think of a child in an age where he or she cannot understand yet the meaning of many words. Try to teach that child the lyrics of a song. Usually, the result of this is you get to teach the child the whole song and even have him or her memorize it. The child can sing it, and he or she can even copy how you pronounce the words, but no matter how the child copies the way you render it, there is still no emotion whatsoever.

This is how a narcissist copies our emotion. They mimic and perfect our expressions and associate them with our emotions. They do all these with the absence of emotions. Since this is quite too easy for them, they tend to get bored by it easily and then they become impassive. This is when a narcissist starts to produce series of inappropriate reactions, all thanks to their impaired yet careful analysis of the normal human's emotions.

Narcissists also use substitution to mask certain emotions and make them appear genuine to the people around him or her. They utilize their short-term and medium-term memory as a storage of reactions, all made-up for his or her supply sources.

A narcissist's reactions are strictly for his supply sources only. Any reactions that need to be produced for someone who does not belong to the narcissist's supply sources will only cause difficulty on the narcissist's end. Remember, a narcissist treats his supply sources as a part of him, thus remembering what sort of reactions this source needs is not a problem for the narcissist. This is because at the end of the day, for the narcissist, the supply sources exist for his existence alone. Anyone who doesn't have any purpose to the narcissist is deemed non-important and maybe even non-existent.

Chapter 4: Possible Causes Of Narcissism

It is extremely hard to pin point at what stage narcissistic tendencies manifest. However, all psychologists agree that narcissism develops from childhood and mutates as a child with emotions that resemble those of a narcissistic adult grow from emotions into character traits. The main three factors include genetics, biological and social. In most cases it is an intertwining of all three.

Narcissism is also known to have roots in genetics and psychobiology. It draws heavily from the connection between the brain, behavior and thinking. So if your family is known for narcissistic traits it is very likely that it may be passed on to you if not curbed properly. At the nurturing phase, we are most likely to emulate the people in our immediate surroundings. Their perspectives and beliefs are bound to have a lasting effect on our character. It may be something as simple as taking after the narcissistic sibling who spends a lot of her time fussing over makeup.

A narcissist is also likely to be born from insecurities that have been buried for too long. Such people may find it absolutely necessary to put on a façade of high self-esteem. This maneuver is usually done to divert attention from the deep sense of insecurity hidden underneath the grand exterior. Nurturing jealousy throughout his/her life, such a person decides that it is about time he was envied as well. His insecurities make him extremely vulnerable to criticism.

Narcissism can also develop from anger management issues wherein an individual has mixed feelings towards how to react in public. These individuals are easily hurt. They prefer not to show it or explode in anger. This tendency gradually forms a self-centered existence that later develops into acute narcissism. The inability to accept defeat or to take responsibility will make the person convince himself that he was right and his peers were at fault.

Inferiority is another major reason for the development of narcissism. As a child if a person is unable to achieve the high standards set by his parents or the society he begins to believe that he is useless and not worth much to anyone. He begins to feel inferior to almost everybody around him as he feels that all of them are have achieved the standards to some degree above his own. He feels threatened in reality and in his own perceptions. These situations ultimately lead to anxiety and depression. When left to battle such a situation alone, the person begins to develop a set of defense mechanisms to protect his own ego. These mechanisms usually involve a voluntary distortion of facts, splitting and projection. A narcissist is born when this person finally develops a superiority complex in response to the mess around him.

Another facet that cements narcissism in an individual is his upbringing. A few unrealistic parenting behaviors may result in setting up a foundation for acute narcissism. There are parents who are extremely permissive. They believe in encouraging their children as much as possible; thus, drawing an unrealistic self-portrait in the child's mind.

The child grows up expecting the rest of the world to treat him the same way his parents did. The harsh and practical world may not laud his "achievements" because as far as they know it was not something worth praise. The person might take some time to come to terms with this sudden change in perspective. He might begin to feel underestimated and useless. All of which fuel his desire to become perfect and worthy of praise.

Parents are expected to set achievable goals for their kids and give them the encouragement they need and nothing more. Idealization is a rare case that happens to very few people. As children, some of us may have had extremely successful and busy parents who might have had to devote more of their time to their career than to their children. In such cases, the child takes it upon himself to make sure that he gains the attention of his parents by excelling at something his parents like.

Along the way, the child sidelines his own dreams and ambitions and focuses on impressing his parents. Without anyone realizing it, the child has already set an unrealistic bar for himself to achieve. This behavior might often result in the person being more concerned with the image he portrays rather than his true self. He might be so obsessed with the image that he would consider it completely normal to promote it even at the cost of his own self. This self usually becomes a shell with a bipolar structure. Its two extremes would be grandiosity at one end and over idealization at the other end. This tendency is also seen when parents use their children to fuel their own ego and image. They make their child a puppet to dance to their tunes.

The child's achievements are used to decorate the parents' image rather than to fuel his ambitions. A narcissistic personality is born to counter this lack of support and encouragement from the parents. Adolescence is that period of time that decides if a child is going to grow up into a narcissist or not. A teenager needs to be handled with care, as they are extremely volatile at that stage. Parents should exercise a level of control and authority over the child without him feeling threatened by it. The teenager should have his own space to grow and should not feel that he is being controlled too much by his authoritative parents. At the same time, a complete lack of guidance or an extremely lenient support from the parents is not advisable either, as it only increases their chances of becoming a narcissist in their adulthood.

When we are young, we are at a constant struggle to develop attitudes that reflect a realistic view of the people and world around us. We are in a constant struggle to develop our God given birth right to become holistic individuals who can accept and give love in equal measures. This holistic being "the real self" or healthy person, is a manifestation of our spirituality and in tandem with God's desire for us. However, and this is where most narcissists are made, to develop into this holistic being, a child must experience certain childhood experiences.

Are you confused? A child is like a clean slate or a blank blackboard; there is nothing there. As the child grows, certain character traits in the parent, or in people around him or her, rub off on the child. In this growth, the child becomes aware of their unique need and abilities.

A good parent recognizes the spiritual, physical, and emotional needs of the child and works to meet them in a healthy manner. The parent lets the child grow into his or her real self without influencing the process by trying to mold the child into what they think is the ideal human being.

Narcissism is a very unhealthy trait. In order for a child to develop the "true self," he or she must experience emotionally sound experiences. On the other hand, emotional distressing situations especially in early childhood is a major cause of narcissistic tendencies and other adjustment disorders. A narcissistic individual fails to develop this true self, and rather than cultivating this true self, he or she works towards developing into someone he thinks people can be proud of or someone everyone will admire.

Additionally, instead of developing the God given strengths and weaknesses, a narcissistic individual is happier when he or she receives affirmation to their perfect but false grandiose self.

As narcissistic tendencies develop in a child, he or she is in a constant search for admiration from other children and peers to what he thinks is his real self but is an unrealistic self-image portrayal. As I have stated, it is almost impossible to pinpoint the exact time normal pride and self-admiration turns into narcissism. However, there are few examples we can look at to see how narcissism forms and what causes it.

In normal degrees, pampering a child is healthy. However, over pampering, letting the child have his or her way every time is unhealthy. On the other hand, neglecting a child or being too intrusive or needy can lead to the development of narcissistic behavior in a child. Overindulgence and spoiling are also a very common parenting behavior. Essentially, the child becomes spoiled in all walks of life. He/she rarely hears the word "no" and is seldom denied what he/she might want, irrespective of whether they need it or not. Such people grow up to believe that the rest of the world merely exists to sustain their wants. Similarly, a spoiled child might expect the same pattern to continue in later life as well.

How so? Over-pampering or being too permissive with a child programs with negative feelings of entitlement and the child might end up feeling superior to other children. In effect, the child fails to develop humility or respect for others mainly because of the failure by the parent in setting boundaries.

Example:

A mother goes to the supermarket with her 7-year-old son; the child sees some candy that he feels he must have oblivious to the grown up world of financial strain, ownership, and health. The child feels that he must have the candy at all cost and if the parent has raised the child right, he accepts that he cannot have the candy. He might throw a tantrum or feel angry at first, but he eventually learns that he cannot have everything he desires. On the other hand, a parent who has raised the child to believe that he is entitled will always indulge the child and in effect, cement the feelings of pride and entitlement.

Children who grow up into narcissistic adults lack the skills to manage their feelings of disappointment and resentment even in early childhood. This ability to manage these feelings "self-soothing" is missing in narcissists.

In addition to the scenarios we have seen, it is also widely speculated that children who grow up in wealthy and influential homes with parents who are not emotionally available lack sensitivity to other people's needs and develop a sense of entitlement.

Recently, therapists and psychologists have concluded that in some cases, the entire family can develop narcissistic tendencies. In a narcissistic family for whatever reason (drug abuse, immaturity, alcoholism etc.), everything revolves around fulfilling the needs of the parent. The children try as much as possible to earn their parent's approval by neglecting their needs and focusing on those of the parent. For this reason, the children lose touch with their peers because they are too busy playing the role of the parent in the family. The child ends up taking the role of a parent, which affects them psychologically. The child suffers emotional damage, and in their desire for the care they never got from their parent, they end up being narcissists who are always in a constant search for admiration. In all these scenarios, one thing is very clear: the effects of a negative upbringing on a child. From childhood, narcissists develop a set of unconscious beliefs. Children can become very perceptive of how the world reacts to them at a very young age. As early as eight years old in some cases. This understanding coupled with a spoiled upbringing that generally makes them see themselves as above everyone else could spark off a narcissistic lifestyle.

Social media is a new trend that has sent levels of narcissism skyrocketing. As if it wasn't enough that narcissism was not doing well enough on its own, social media sites like Facebook and Instagram have provided a platform for narcissists to stand out. With the invention of selfies, narcissistic pictures and lifestyle have definitely been on the rise. Teenagers with smartphones spend a lot of their time wondering when and where to click their next profile picture. The constant battle on the internet to have the most trending picture has seen people dedicatedly trying to outdo the rest by taking pictures of themselves in the most bizarre and sometimes even risky places. Every time someone "likes" a person's photo, it fuels that person to raise the bar and try to outdo himself. The "suaveness" of a person has come down to being completely dependent on the number of likes he/she manages to accumulate every time they change their profile picture. The fact that celebrities update their profiles with similar photographs every hour or so, do not help matters. The adolescents do their best to emulate their role models and indulge in narcissistic practices. With the release of applications like Snapchat that do not allow a picture to be viewed for more than a few seconds, a lot of introverts have also begun embracing narcissism willingly. Social media and its benefits are not necessarily a twenty first century evil but they have to be used sensibly and responsibly.

In some extreme cases, narcissism is seen as an invocation wherein an individual's normal personality is substituted for another. While some people see this as being possessed by a god or a deity, others see the narcissist as being under demonic possession.

In the next chapter, we shall look at some of the most common characteristics of a narcissist.

Chapter 5: Identifying Narcissist Characteristics And Common Traits

There are many indicators used to identify a narcissist, but this is not to say that everyone displaying these behaviors is suffering from narcissism. Remember narcissism is a psychological disorder and as so, other psychological disorders may manifest through the same characteristics as those displayed by a narcissist. The characteristics we shall look at can give you further insight into the mind of a narcissist, which can be very helpful when you are dealing with someone suffering from the condition.

Fear of Rejection

A narcissist is usually suffering from an emotional trauma. He harbors fears of rejection. In fact, more than anything else, this is the one thing he fears the most in the world. He or she is highly attuned to anything that he (for all intents and purpose, he should be taken to mean the narcissist person) considers signs of impending rejection. He believes that rejection is a shameful thing that is an experience only for the weak. He builds a wall around him and does not let anyone close. He believes that he can be rejected or disappointed only if he piles up too much hope on someone. He tends to value material things like wealth more than relationships and will literally be more in love with material things than actual people. He will cheat, manipulate, and lie to protect himself and keep people from glimpsing the weak person he knows himself to be. He builds up a façade and makes himself accept it as a reality, refusing to see the real world without his filter. With a self-proclaimed sense of importance he fails to see the logic behind why a person like him would ever have to hear a "no". If he was brought up as a spoilt brat he is used to having his way all the time and goes into depression and anxiety when something doesn't go his way.

Have a False Self

We have already seen that a child raised in what society considers a normal, healthy home setting develops into his true self. A child brought up in an unhealthy home on the other hand, does not get this chance. He spent his entire childhood trying to grow into someone else's shoes that he did not bother finding his own. Be it an over achiever kid constantly trying to impress his parents or a rowdy teenager who goes out of his way to disappoint his family, every potential narcissist develops a false identity or self. At times they may also become mildly schizophrenic which may fully develop into multiple personalities later on. He thinks that the only person who is truly capable of appreciating him is himself. It shouldn't be surprising if he discusses most of his problems with his other self or imaginary friend. In this way, he also justifies having looked at a problem from different angles. Therefore, he grows up without knowing who he truly is. He develops a false self and because he is in a desperate search for what he thinks is the ideal love, he is unable to connect intimately with anyone. Love and affection may hit him right in the face but he may not realize it because he is constantly in search of the extraordinary. This is mainly because of his fear for betrayal, rejection, and abandonment. He does not let anyone get too close to him and maintains a distance from everyone.

Additionally, because he does not really know himself and hides behind his false self, it is impossible for anyone to get close enough to form a substantive relationship with him. People who do get close enough are hurt and sent off in such a way that they wouldn't even consider rekindling the relationship again. Moreover, because of his entitlement, he is capable of one selfless act "any act directed at himself" which is not unlike the Greek mythology of Narcissus.

Have a Narcissistic Circle

Due to his desire to be around people who he thinks worship or admire him, he will have a circle. Imagine the most popular kid in high school. He is likely to have his own band of followers who hang out with him all the time. Either out of respect or to prevent themselves from being picked on. The narcissistic circle is somewhat similar. This circle consists of people who constantly remind the narcissist that he is the greatest thing that happened to the world. They add fuel to his already burning ego-fire. This circle comprises of people who are termed as Narcissist supply.

Narcissist supply is a group of people who provide the narcissist with the approval, attention and admiration he craves. The false self in the narcissist needs this supply source and he deems it necessary for his survival. Because of this constant barrage of admiration, either false or otherwise, the narcissist's ego inflates like an air balloon. He depends on this steady stream of admiration and attention to feed his ego. Unknown to himself, he begins to depend on this circle more than he would like to admit. When looking at the big picture it reminds us of the bully and his band of cowards who simply use the bigger kid for protection and in return laugh at any joke he makes.

The narcissistic supply circle is no better than the narcissist himself, and because the narcissist is determined to get to the top of his position to get recognition, the supply circle will use the narcissist need for attention to advance their own agenda; be it a promotion at work or special treatment. In most cases, the narcissist is too obsessed with himself to realize that he is being played until it is too late. The circle may have people who might be clever but not as popular or well known as the narcissist. So they cunningly make use of his talents to fuel their own agenda while pacifying the narcissist simultaneously. He sincerely believes that the narcissistic circle simply exists to praise and goad his achievements.

On the other hand, the narcissist is quick to point out to himself that he does not need anyone and the only reason people admire him and offer his praise is because they really feel that way about him. It does not cross his mind that those people might have an ulterior motive and may not be doing the whole thing out of admiration. The narcissist decides that he has to be the center of attention for his supply circle and will not tolerate independence from anyone in the circle. He is firmly rooted in the belief that the circle is there to serve him. Any signs of noncompliance with the needs of the narcissist from anyone in the circle will send him into a rage. He can be quick to anger and his temper is not worth invoking because beyond that line he completely ceases to see all logic and will not calm down until he has had his revenge.

Rage

The narcissist is a very angry person. He uses this rage to scream for the attention he craves. He will scream at anyone in the office because of mundane things. When his narcissistic false self is injured, prepare to see a side of him that is mostly well veiled. When what he considers a narcissistic injury (a threat to his well-cultivated false self, self-esteem and worth) occurs, his rage comes spewing out like an angry volcano. While the rage is raging on, the narcissist is contemplating only one thing, revenge. To a person who thinks he is always right, a narcissist has an ego that cannot be satiated. So when someone puts him or his actions in the wrong he retaliates in the most violent matter. Rage can also be a publicity stunt for him, where he screams his head off just so that a couple of people turn around and acknowledge that he is a big shot. It is very important to differentiate between anger and narcissistic rage.

Traditional anger triggers or situations that demand for the emotional response of anger do not provoke narcissistic rage. Normal anger is usually incited when someone hurts us or our loved ones or when we see an open act of injustice on an oppressed individual. Normal anger although a bad trait is selfless in its own way. A person is able to see beyond his own problems and stand up for others. A narcissist's rage is his way of scarring people, and when he sees fear on their faces, to him, it is a signal that he has won. This fear fuels their sadistic nature and cements their feelings of importance. It makes no difference to a narcissist that the people around him are getting hurt or unjustly treated. In fact, he might even turn a blind eye on such incidents. His rage is completely invoked only when his physical or emotional self has been hurt. He might go to unreasonable fits of rage if so much as a fingernail on his person is broken but remains completely indifferent if someone is being beaten to death. Due to this rage, the narcissist has no friends or anyone that you and I (normal folks) would call a close friend. In his delusional state, a narcissist thinks that the rage is his way of gaining back his control. His open display of unreasonable rage is his way of exercising control on his personal space and domain.

Need For Control and power

The life of a narcissist has one major driver, domination. He is basically a control freak who would willingly exercise control over the air we breathe if it were up to him. As a person who has problems with rejection, he tries to influence anything and everything around him. When asked for advice, he provides it willingly and follows up on it. He will make sure the person follows his advice to the letter and will not allow him to deviate from his suggestion. When asked for an opinion or small suggestion he expects the person to dissolve any other ideas he might have had and religiously follow the one that the narcissist provided. A narcissist lives to dominate everything he touches; his workplace, every person he interacts with, and social events. He does not look at power as "power with" but looks at it as "power over". He uses power and control as his springboard for emotional and verbal abuse. He enjoys being able to look down on people and stepping on them from time to time. Although narcissists have good control over power from a practical point of view, that level of control is not something the other people would look forward to. When in the driver's seat, the narcissist would be the only one enjoying the ride. He has opinions on the correct way of doing things, either at home or at work. However, when it comes to the actual implementation of the plan, he has no desire to be hands on. He believes he is too precious for menial work. So although he has opinions on every small detail, he will not be bothered to burn calories over any of it. He firmly decides that the whole thing will go smoothly only if he is placed in the manager's chair. His idea of control would be to constantly nag people about not doing their work properly. When one of his colleagues does finish their work on time and in a very good way, he gives them credit for it half-heartedly.

For example, in a home situation, he is very financially restrictive, which leaves him to control the entire expenditure. He thinks that every basic need of the family has to pass through him and wants people to ask him for permission before they do anything. He is extremely happy when people ask him for permission to do something. In fact, he thinks it is downright outrageous that people would leave him out of the loop. He is quick to condemn anyone he thinks is not doing something the correct way, his way. He reluctantly gives credit when deserved, and complains through the whole process idea. In his delusion, he believes that ultimately, he deserves all the praise because to him, the success of the plan is because of him. His ideology entitles him to the full credit behind the success of any plan he was involved in, even if his contribution was close to nothing. On the other hand, if the plan fails, it is the fault of junior officers and not him. Just as good as he is at taking credit for things he didn't do, he is equally agile at throwing the blame on others for something that might have been entirely his fault.

Seeks Grandiosity

This is the most outstanding and most discriminating feature of any narcissist. His perspective at life shows him in an awesome light and the others on a level beneath him. A narcissist convinces himself that he is one of the most important people on the planet. He believes that the events that led up to his life since his birth has some grand reason or phenomenal divine planning behind it. He has an unrealistic overvaluation of his abilities and talents. Regardless of how talented he might be, a narcissist always tends to over sell himself by exaggerating his abilities. The superiority complex kicks in and he decides that all his abilities and skills are the best that anyone can get. He is preoccupied with himself, fantasies of power, success, beauty, and believes that he is superior and unique. Due to this, he is boastful, self-centered, pretentious, and self-referential. He lives a lot in dreams, where he glorifies his existence in such a grand manner that he has to build up a façade of grandiosity just to make his reality worth living.

In the archives of general psychiatry, the narcissist exaggerates his abilities, achievements, talents, and capacity to cover his lack thereof. Admitting that he lacks certain skill sets that a rival or fellow worker might have hurts his ego so he exaggerates to a very dangerous level. Sky is the limit for such self-wound fantasies. He believes that he has no limitations and due to his grandiose fantasies, he believes that he does not need anyone.

Cannot Handle Shame

To the narcissist, there is a fine line between his perfectionism and grandiosity. He feels inadequate when he fails to get something he wants. Rejection, lack of control over his surroundings and a lack of attention may also bring about this sense of uselessness. Coincidentally, when the narcissist experiences shame, he feels inferior and full of flaws. This causes injuries to his narcissistic false self. In spite of all the grand build up, there are times when a narcissist has to accept reality. In most cases, this reality is accompanied by shame and an inferiority complex. This stark contrast to his perfect fantasy world is a huge emotional blow to the narcissist. He becomes extremely volatile and unpredictable. At this stage, he is in a complete rage directing the anger at anyone in his vicinity. He feels inadequate, exposed, and vulnerable and this overwhelms him. So to vent out this negative energy, he turns viciously onto the people in his immediate vicinity. The reason or logic behind the rage may or may not be justified. As far as he is concerned, he tries to call away the attention from his inferior self by indulging in mindless acts of violence.

Seeks Perfectionism

A narcissist is obsessive, and the false self governs his obsession. This obsession over perfection and method entitle him to produce better quality work than his peers. He sets unachievable and downright impossible goals to achieve. Due to his unrealistic goals and grandiosity, he is always struggling to reach and accomplish goals and feels a lot of shame when he cannot. The tasks that he set for himself may be beyond normal human capacity but he cannot process failure as something that might have happened to anybody. He pressurizes himself into believing that even the most fouled plan will work if he is in charge of it because of his superiority and uniqueness. He also believes that even if other people are able to pull it off, they can never do it with his mind blowing level of perfection.

Additionally, because the narcissist thinks in the lines of "all right or all wrong" (no middle ground) or all "white and black", all his achievements have to be either of the one ways. He does not believe in a compromise. All his results and achievements have to be a soaring success or it is deemed as a failure. Accomplishments that fall short of his grandiosity are complete failures in his sights, and because he thinks he knows everything there is to know in his field of study, he has no room for learning. He will not accept that he has room for improvement, as he is already perfect in every aspect. Every project he undertakes has to be a "eureka" moment or to him, it is a complete failure. He might be able to take a project to a sixty percent success but he will not consider that an achievement, he will drop the entire idea and start on something else in search of that one path breaking moment. When that moment happens, he is extremely elated and boastful about it that he will speak about it for years. This "eureka" moment stokes his ego.

When he does not achieve his goals, his sense of perfectionism and uniqueness feels compromised. He feels devalued, shameful, and vulnerable. Failure enrages him and fills him with self-loath and doubt. He will reprimand himself, which in turn will stroke his rage. When he falls short of his perfectionist tendencies, he experiences a great deal of shame as an ongoing tug of war between balancing grandiosity and perfectionism. Each failure makes him more unstable than he already is. So if a narcissist has been failing continuously or quite some time then his chances of losing his sanity are very high.

Frequently Bored

The narcissist is in a constant never-ending search for excitement in his life. He uses the excitement to feel good about himself. A narcissist is an adrenaline junkie. They will definitely jump off the plane or do a bungee jump; they will chase all kinds of thrills in the hope that it will cement their uniqueness and help ease the rage they may always have. He is in a never ending search for new thrills. No hobby can hold him down as it is only a matter of time before he gets bored of it.

They are extremely aggressive and when faced with boredom, the narcissist will plummet into despair. He will do everything to avoid this despair because it brings with it those feelings of helplessness, despair, and a need for love and admiration. When faced with absolutely nothing to do and no one to turn to, he may also begin actively indulging in degrading addictive practices. He is always willing to explore something new just to rid himself of boredom. Whether the practice in question has a negative effect on him is only secondary as his primary objective is to keep himself busy. From a third person's point of view it does make sense to keep a narcissist occupied; preferably with some harmless activity to keep him off the streets. His uncontrolled flow of emotion is most likely to endanger himself and others around him.

To the narcissistic person, boredom creates anxiety and siphons out every bit of their morale. For this very reason, the narcissist will not tolerate boredom for long. If their narcissistic supply chain is not available, you will find the narcissist performing activities that attract a lot of attention to him. Just as much as he craves to be the center of attention, he is sufficiently equipped to grab the attention for himself.

Constantly Seeking Fame

The narcissist is always looking for glory. He will do

anything to be in the limelight because to him, being in the limelight is proof of acceptance and admiration from his peers. All this is in the hope that the fame and subsequent admiration will help fill the emptiness from childhood that cannot go away.

The constant need for admiration is because of the intolerable need for human contact he lacked as a child or the sense of entitlement he developed as a child. Due to the constant struggle between his true and false self, the narcissist will suffer from multiple personality disorder. When he is feeling shame, out of control, or inadequate, he will split off to the personality that he feels safe in.

A point to note here is that while the narcissist will experience shame, the shame is not specifically directed at himself, rather outwards, towards other people rather than the self. This is so that he can preserve the self from taking responsibility or experiencing any backlash such as unworthiness or self-contempt. To elevate these feelings when they creep up, the narcissist will retreat to his narcissistic supply or place themselves in a situation they are bound to receive a lot of praise for whatever reason. The fame makes him feel alive, wanted, and desired.

The more desired he feels, the more grandiose he gets, and the more arrogant he gets. While he is being celebrated, he takes this to be an affirmation of his importance, or rather, the importance of his fake self. He gets overly confident and verbose and he will go to great lengths to display his newly found celebrity status. At this stage of his self-assuredness and self-confidence, the narcissist operated at the illusion that crossing him in the wrong way will lead to retribution.

Chapter 6: The Different Types Of Narcissism

While we talk about narcissism in general terms, there is more than one type. In the real world, when you meet a narcissist face to face, there may be signs that matches the way a narcissist behave because most of the time, they are a mix of the various types. As with typical mixes, there is always the dominant type mix with another.

To help you to determine which one is what, here's a brief rundown of each different type and their specific characteristics or personality traits:

Cerebral

A cerebral narcissist believes that they are better than anyone and that their intelligence far exceeds that of anyone else. They flaunt their intelligence and self-assumed superiority to be admired and envied by the rest. They know everything about, well, everything. They make it a point to have an opinion or suggestion for everything that you might throw at them. They will be happy to tell you stories that show off their sheer brilliance, whether the stories are real or just made up. They are happy to point out everyone else's failings and will look down on and sneer at anyone who is of a lower intelligence. Such people are so obsessed with their grey matter that they will go out of their way to take alarmingly good care of it, sometimes to an extent that it reflects badly on their health and physical prowess. Narcissism is very often associated with sexual stimulation. Cerebral narcissists rarely engage in sexual stimulation with others, as they prefer personal stimulation over the real deal. Therefore, it would not come as much of a surprise when I say that they prefer the anonymity and lack of intimacy that comes with pornography. For this reason they may choose porn over close real relationships. Besides maintaining a relationship with such people is a Herculean task in itself. As they will always insist on being the intellectually superior one in the relationship and assumes the right to control the other person's thoughts, emotions and actions. Even then, these relationships will be extremely short lived as they are constantly looking for more superior people to associate with. Cerebral narcissists should not be confused with somatic narcissists.

Somatic

Somatic narcissists are more closely in touch with the Greek legend of Narcissus. They are all consumed by how beautiful they believe they are. You will often find somatic narcissists at a gym or somewhere else where they are working on their appearance. For them it is all about their body and physique. They can be constantly seen flexing their muscles and bragging about their success in sporting events. They expect their body to be the source of their narcissistic supply and so they dress up immaculately and keep themselves well groomed. Their narcissistic supply comes from how others react to how they look or from their sexual conquests – indeed, most somatic narcissists will have a long list of partners. They never cease to boast about their conquests in bed. Even though they may have bedded a lot of partners, most of the sex is bound to be cold and emotionless. Eventually, the word partner begins to lose meaning and they may be more aptly described as the victim. Cheating in a marital life is something that you shouldn't put past a somatic narcissist. He is happiest when his narcissistic supply comes from multiple sources. They are quite dangerous as they know how to manipulate people both emotionally and through sexual intercourse. This tends to scar their spouse for life if they decide to be in a long term relationship with them.

Overt

This form of narcissism manifests grandiosity. They are preoccupied about having outstanding success in a lot of areas, like brilliance, attractiveness, sense of power, ideal love etc. Since they have a large sense of grandiosity, they believe that they can only be fully appreciated by other people on their level of grandiosity. The overt narcissist always has to be in control of any situation. They are never wrong and they will never be shy about making it clear that everything is about them and that everything has to be done the way they want it done. Their egos are super-sized and they are not backwards in showing it to you either. The overt narcissist is able to cut you up, physically or verbally and will not show a single second of remorse or guilt. Such people are interpersonally very exploitative and will not think twice before using someone to achieve their own needs. Although very arrogant on the inside, they are experts at masking their egotism within a false humility. They envy other people to a great extent and get terribly jealous of their achievements, possessions and relationships. They seriously lack empathy and this makes them unfit to work in a group. They are usually loners.

They may be seen as being overconfident and they are definitely extrovert in their behavior – in fact, it would easier to describe their personality as loud, obvious, larger than life, and somewhat oppressive.

Covert

The covert narcissist exhibits all the normal traits you would expect to find in a narcissist but with one difference – they want someone to take care of them. They are best described as the shy form of narcissism. He has grand fantasies similar to other types of narcissists but he lacks the drive to pull it off successfully. He is too timid to get what he wants and lacks self-confidence. He usually feels worthless at not being able to pull off exactly what he wanted. He faces large feelings of shame about the same thing. He rarely takes credit for his achievements. He openly admires successful people and secretly envies them. He is unlikely to accumulate appropriate friends and prefers to surround himself with more inferior type of people. Such people are hyper vigilant to rejection and humiliation. They could be described as parasites, living off other people. They will normally exhibit some signs of an illness that needs taking care of and that is why they can never be what you want. They don't want to take responsibility for anything and will look for a partner who is strong, successful, and intelligent, one that can run their lives while they don't need to contribute anything. Covert narcissists will sometimes pair up with the overt narcissist.

Unprincipled

The unprincipled narcissist does not have a conscience and cannot seem to tell the difference between what's right and what's wrong. They care very little about laws, values and conventions and stay just within the boundaries of the law. They exploit others without the slightest bit of remorse because they consider other people as inferior to them anyway. This unprincipled lifestyle makes them more than willing to risk harm and they are remarkable fearless in the face of danger. Their malicious and diabolic tendencies are easily visible and they get them into trouble with the department of law. They achieve gratification by dominating and humiliating others. These people never form an allegiance with anyone and so move from person to person with remarkable ease. They are alien to emotional attachments and do not feel the slightest remorse on ending a very promising relationship. The people they leave crumpled in their wake are very adversely affected, as the narcissist is usually very charming. These narcissists are exceptionally dangerous because for them, truth is only relative. They are masters of manipulation and deceit. They are very adept at scheming beneath a polite and civil veneer. Their plans are usually very cunning and worthy of admiration even though the means is hardly justified. They show no concern for other people's welfare, have no morals, scruples, and are highly deceptive when they deal with others. They will give off an air of arrogance and are driven by a need to get the better of everyone, just to prove that they are smarter. This kind of narcissist may be found in prisons or drug rehabilitation centers although there are an awful lot of unprincipled narcissists who never come up against the law. When in the vicinity of an unprincipled narcissist always be sure to keep your guard up. They smell insecurities a mile away and can easily turn you into a scapegoat for their next exploit.

Amorous

Amorous narcissists tend to be erotic or seductive in nature and they measure their entire self-worth around their, sometimes many, sexual conquests. Their relationships are often pathological and, as soon as they seduce someone, they are likely to throw them to one side while they look for their next conquest. They are never looking for an emotional connect but rather seek to inflate their already bloated ego by sexually dominating other people who they consider as trophies. The victim has more or less no idea that they are being used and sometimes they sincerely fall in love with the narcissists. However, the narcissist sincerely lacks any empathy and will simply throw them away like paper towels. This makes them outrageous heartbreakers. Not only are they often known as heartbreakers, they will also do some outrageous things, like pathological lying, conning their sexual partner out of money and other fraudulent acts. They use their sexual prowess to con unsuspecting people. The amorous narcissist is compensation for deep feelings of inadequacy. In most cases, they get away with it too because people hesitate to lodge a complaint against them.

Compensatory

Compensatory narcissists are constantly looking for a way to compensate for things that happened in the past, perhaps in their childhood and they do this by creating an illusion that they are superior. They tend to live in a fantasy world where they play the leading role in a theater that doesn't exist rather than living a real life. They imagine achievements in a bid to enhance their own self-esteem. They need an audience filled with people who will believe their deceptions and they are extremely sensitive to how other people perceive them, looking for signs that they are being criticized. They literally try to compensate for everything that they feel they were deprived off. Their agenda is similar to the other narcissists except that they are more focused rather than being guilty of random acts of narcissism.

Elite

The elite narcissist is, in many ways, very similar to the compensatory narcissist in that they are obsessed with their own self-image. The sense of self they create rarely resembles the real person but they manage to convince themselves and others that they have unique abilities and talents. They will, more often than not, turn a relationship into a contest or a competition where the only goal is to win, to prove to others that they are truly superior. This will happen with any type of relationship, be it family, work, or love. The elite narcissist is a social climber and will be happy to step on anyone who gets in his or her way. In a way, he is the most dangerous of all the types as he hides in plain sight so effectively that even the ones closest to him perceive him as a good and honest person. An elite narcissist is usually a highly successful businessman or business woman who has a very reputable profile. They consider material wealth and assets as a primary objective over true emotion. They are masters of deception and often use their talents to walk over other people. Being as cunning as they get, they usually have a legitimate and reputed business that they use as a front for all of their shady dealings. They are extremely protective of their personal space. If they get the slightest hint that you are a threat to everything that they have built up they will eliminate you without a second thought. They are ruthless and without remorse or empathy. They are concerned only with their well being and the achievement of their goals. They will go to any length to achieve what they want.

Below are some of the narcissistic sub-types. These sub-types can be encountered from various people on a daily basis. Some can be annoying but tolerated, while some can cause emotional harm.

Conversational

Ever recall an instance where you are talking to a certain person, ranting or just randomly telling one of your everyday life stories to him? What's unforgettable is how the conversation always manages to end up with ***him*** as the subject and the victor? Annoying, right? Not only is it sickening to hear stories with always the same triumphant result, it is also annoying that they always make you forget what you are about to say due to their constant *interruption.*

This kind of conversation can happen between normal people as well, but it is almost always the case with people suffering from narcissism. There is even more aggressive conversational narcissist where they rudely cut you off while you were saying something, just so they can insist their own story whose lead character is always them.

If, by reading this part of the book, you are reminded of that one person who never fails to do this each and every time you are having a conversation, try to observe. Check out his other mannerisms, habits, or the way he behaves with other people Chances are, you have a narcissist who is sneakily turning all his friends into his supply sources.

Group Narcissism

Whenever the topic is narcissism, we are always presented with the idea that it is all about a person who cares for nothing else but ***himself.*** This is true, but it does not necessarily rule out the possibility of narcissism that can occur in a group.

In group narcissism, the narcissist individual is always a part of the group. Usually, the group is made up of narcissist people who mirror themselves and doesn't encounter any problem with having to co-exist with each other. They tend to become the narcissist supply source of each other and you will know that it is working out as the group acts as a narcissistic entity.

You see, narcissists have the tendency to gather or join each other in groups because it brings them comfort. This is due to the fact that they are all, pretty much, similar and share the same behaviors or habits. There's no questioning about why he behaves this way and she behaves that way, because they all know that they are trying to protect someone deep inside them.

Now, this group becomes a protector of the hidden *real selves* of each member. While this looks nice and beneficial for narcissist, this does not mean that they are already safe from the danger of self-destruction. It's always there, just below the surface.

Aggressive or Malignant Narcissism

This type of narcissism is your lesser type (like classic, cerebral, somatic, elite, and others) kicked up a notch because it becomes violent and psychopathic.

Remember Adolf Hitler or Ted Bundy? They are categorized as aggressive types of narcissists.

Not all narcissists prefer to physically harm their supply source or victims. Most of the time, they just torture or abuse you mentally. However, when a narcissist becomes a bit too physical and performs murder, rape, or some other crimes with cold blood, that person can already be categorized as a malignant or aggressive narcissist.

Destructive Narcissism

So we have labels for, pretty much, every type of narcissist out there. Honestly, some psychiatrists do not exactly agree with these labels because identifying a narcissist is more than just knowing all the types and matching the several behaviors or signs dominant to that type.

What is more, there are also narcissists who are too clever that they are able to compensate for some of the behaviors in order to cover them up. That way, lesser track means lesser disruption to the facade that took them years and so much lies to build and complete.

There are also some people who cannot be also classified as a narcissist, but confuses you because they really match some of a narcissist's description. Now, why am I saying all these? This is because this type, the destructive narcissist, is one of those who do not technically fit the definition of a narcissist, but they also inflict plain on themselves and also shows general narcissist patterns.

Out of all the types, the destructive narcissist is the one that seems to be a bit irregular. It has some of the traits that can easily identify them within the various types of narcissist and all the while lacks some narcissistic traits that will solidify their being categorized as a narcissist.

Destructive narcissists usually have the most intense characteristics that a narcissist can have. These characteristics are set to ruin and destruct people around the narcissist and because of this, you can easily associate them with a pathological narcissist. However, the mentioned characteristics are fewer.

Sexual Narcissism

While this may raise your eyebrows as we have come to know that narcissists aren't exactly crazy about having sex with someone else, let us take a quick look at who these sexual narcissists are. Sex, when blended with grandiose becomes sexual narcissism. A sexual narcissist boasts pleasurable sexual skills, has sexual entitlement, and he also lacks sexual empathy.

The meaning? You get to have an intercourse with a sexual narcissist, but as always, it is for his pleasure and not yours. You may feel a satisfaction and this is no wonder because of the sexual skills of the narcissist. However, if the narcissist feels that he is already satisfied and you aren't yet, even if you are right in the middle of it and he wants to stop, he will stop.

He will only do it with you when he feels like it. So if a sexual narcissist doesn't feel like doing it, even if two weeks has passed already, you will never get one.

Another thing that you have to know about the sexual narcissist is that they have a big tendency to be an unfaithful partner. Big surprise! Since they feel like they have all the sexual skills, they also feel that they can do it with anyone as long as they are in the mood for it.

Acquired Situational Narcissism (ASN)

This narcissism sub-type is a lot different from the rest of the types, even the main ones, as ASN is acquired later on in life as an adult. All other narcissism types are acquired in the childhood phase of a person's life.

ASN can't just happen to anyone. One needs to have the narcissistic tendency as a child for ASN to be successfully triggered. This type of narcissism is triggered when an adult with narcissistic tendency suddenly comes across wealth, celebrity-status, or fame. Through this, the previous tendency suddenly blooms into a full-blown narcissistic personality disorder complete with signs, symptoms, behaviors and more harmful probabilities like the usual type of narcissism. The only difference is the age when the sufferer acquired it.

What feeds their narcissistic cravings are their fans, supporters, people around them, their fake friends, assistants, social media, and the traditional type of media.

Chapter 7: Treatment And Management Of Narcissism

Now that you know some common characteristics of the narcissist, how do you deal with a narcissist and how can you treat the condition?

The best long-term approach to curing narcissism is long-term outpatient care. There are no pills specifically dedicated to narcissism. However, as we have seen, narcissism is a psychological problem, and like many psychological problems, there are treatments available with a subscription from a licensed psychologist.

Ideally, the treatment for narcissism is managed

medication and psychotherapy, more specifically, psychoanalytic psychotherapy. This does not mean there are no other methods that work in its management and treatment. Due to its close relation to family problems, most psychotherapists will suggest using family groups, couples therapy, and cognitive behavioral therapy.

Additionally, a psychotherapist may choose to use focused short-term psychotherapy. As I have hinted, there is no all-out pill specifically designed for NPD (narcissistic personality disorder). The psychotherapist may decide to use his or her discretion to prescribe psychotropic medication to treat anxiety, impulsivity, depression and many more psychologically related mood disturbances.

In most cases, outpatient is the best mode of treatment. However, in instance where the narcissist is a danger to himself or those around him, the psychotherapist may opt for inpatient treatment. The inpatient treatments are short because prolonged hospital stay undermines the treatment process. How so? Longer hospital stays will make the narcissist experience all the feeling he has been trying to bottle up before he has developed the coping mechanism required as he under gradual treatment. An inpatient treatment should only allow for enough time for mood stabilization or correct medication dosage.

There is no ideal way to treat narcissism; if you realize that you are living with a narcissist or are a narcissist, the best thing is to visit a psychotherapist for diagnosis and treatment. With this in mind, there are a few things believed to help someone associate better with a known narcissist.

Managing someone with narcissistic tendencies will require a lot of ingenuity, understanding, and fortitude, as well as an understanding of their characteristics so that you can use their self-importance to cope with them.

* Firstly, if you are in a work situation, remember that narcissists like to be associated with power. Keep your distance. If you are superior to him, demand respect.

Show them that with one phone call, you can easily report them to the management of the firm and make sure to hint at the fact that all top management knows you by name and vice versa.

* Narcissists are not what you would consider team players. If you are working on a project that requires team play choose the people who work best as a team and give the narcissist a solo project. If you do not have a solo project, place the narcissist in a team that constitutes his equals and peers, or people he admires. Additionally, due to their belief that they are superior or unique, a narcissist will ask for special favors. Do not afford him this luxury. Stick to the rules. Do not bend the rules for him or give in to their unrealistic demands.

* Remember what we said earlier, narcissists are always seeking for glory. If a narcissist steps forward to take the glory for a successful project done by you, step forward and do not allow him to take away all the glory for your project.

Chapter 8: Five Things To Avoid When Dealing With A Narcissist

It is very easy to lose yourself in a narcissist's world, either by argument. It is also very easy to be drawn in by his grandiose nature. Here are five things to avoid when dealing with a narcissist.

#- Never ever allow yourself to get into an argument with a narcissist. Remember what we have looked at. A narcissist will go into a rage if you contradict him. He will use this rage to fuel his self-importance. Do not give him the pleasure. Also, his rage is not managed. There is no predicting what he will do to hurt you and get the upper hand. Even if he is downright wrong about something, always remember that you have nothing to gain from winning the bout. It would be more prudent to change the subject and divert his attention.

#- If you can avoid it, never offer a narcissist any intimacy. As we have seen, narcissists are emotionally incapable of connecting with anyone. Offering him or her any intimacy is like hanging your heart out on your chest for the birds to peck on. He will size up your paltry offer and use it for his own entertainment. You will mean nothing more to him than any other doll he could purchase at a local toy store. The suave and polite charm may throw you off guard but keep a professional distance in the interest of your own welfare.

#- Never show awe or interest in his grandiose achievement. We have already established that narcissists are chronic exaggerators. They will make a swim in the pool seem like a swim across the channel. Showing awe or amazement in his achievement will only fuel his grandiosity and lies. Lauding his most simple achievements will gain you only one thing; a VIP pass into his narcissistic circle, where you are expected to hang on to his every word and praise him even when you don't want to.

#- Narcissists live in their own grandiose world: let him be. Do not try to remove him from this world in any way. If you have to refer to the world out there (read the real world), try to connect this with his grandiosity. If you so much as threaten his world he will retaliate in a way that you cannot handle. He will tear your world down with all his rage and cunning if you as much as scratch at his protective bubble.

#- No matter what you do, do not make any comment that you think will compromise his self-proclaimed importance. Try to avoid using some of these lines when you are talking to him:

*You overlooked...

*You made a mistake...

*I think that you do not know...

*You must not...

*You cannot...

In general, avoid any sentences that might make him feel intimidated. The reason for this is simply that you do not want their rage directed at you because it is very easy for narcissistic rage to turn into something else (a fight). An intimidated narcissist is like a cobra backed into a corner. There is no telling what kind of trouble you might find yourself in.

Chapter 9: Getting The Upper Hand: Making A Narcissist Depend On You

If you have tried everything to no avail, it is time to get the upper hand. Due to their vulnerable nature, it is not extremely difficult to make a narcissist dependent on you. Beneath all the tough façade, his emotional vulnerability is every narcissist's Achilles' heel. This is helpful when you do not have any other choice other than to live with him. We will have a look at how you can make the narcissist depend on you.

#- Hang on his every word. Attentively listen to whatever he has to say no matter how grandiose it seems, and of course, agree with him. Even if his account seems far-fetched and poorly scripted, hear him out and nod your head. Agreeing with him does not mean that you believe what he says; it simply means that you know better than to question or start an argument with him.

#- Offer him something that he cannot find anywhere else. This will require some ingenuity on your part. Find out what he craves for, what he deems to be most important and offer this to him. The problem with this is that the more you give the more a narcissist demands. If you absolutely must live with him, keep it coming. It will not be very difficult. Use their grandiosity and their flair for the dramatic to your advantage and consistently find out what makes their hearts tick.

#- Patience, patience, and more patience. Go out of way to be accommodative. This will allow you into his "narcissistic supply" group. This will help keep the rage at bay and subsequently, afford you some peace of mind.

#- Become Mother Teresa. Give, give, and then give some more. Remember that narcissists are very dependent on praise and admiration so if you can consistently provide this, you are in his good graces.

#- Isolate yourself from their emotions and finances. Isolating yourself emotionally can be helpful in those instances, where in his rage, the narcissist says something hurtful. Mostly, use the silent treatment on him with words like, "We will talk later when you are back to your senses".

Financial freedom on the other hand is self-explanatory. Your narcissist will want to control the finances so that he can control you. Be independent from him in case one day he decides to storm out on you. Narcissists exercise control mainly through financial dependence. Have a rainy day account in case he decides to pull the plug in a fit of rage.

#- If you are those people who like to fix situations, do not think that the narcissist is a fixer. The narcissist, especially an adult narcissist is incapable of changing not because they cannot change, but because they have no desire to change. Do not delude yourself; simply accept him for who he is. It might be something of an achievement to pull one over a narcissist and make him see sense but it is sincerely not worth any of the effort at all.

#- If you must fix him, do not do it in a negative way. The best way to fix him is by gradually helping him realize his problem. It is of utmost importance that you perform this task without any negative emotion otherwise; your narcissist will rebel and withdraw into his cocoon. Think of it like living with a handicapped person and being able to discuss the handicap in an unemotional manner. The treatment to any psychological disorder always begins with making the victim realize that there is something wrong with him. Realization is the first step to recovery. Put it across subtly. Narcissists are known to not react well to drastic change.

#- More important than all the above is that you must know yourself. Why are you attracted to him? Are you codependent? Are you masochist? What are you benefiting from the relationship? Answering these questions will help you develop strategies to secure your safety, especially in situations where your narcissist is very angry. Make sure you know what you want and arrange your priorities.

Chapter 10: Seven Steps – How To Break Free From A Narcissist

When you decide that enough is enough and you need to free yourself from the narcissistic abuse you have been suffering, it's helpful to have some guidelines to follow. This is not going to be easy; it is not like breaking apart a "normal" relationship and you will go through some tough times. Besides splitting away from a control freak is not an easy task. As if it is not hard enough already the narcissistic individual will only make it living hell for you.

You may find that you have no energy. You will feel as though you are alone, that you are worthless and you will feel an intense rejection but, believe me, sticking to your guns will pull you through this and you can come out the other side in one piece. Without further ado, let's get started.

Step 1 – Say Goodbye

When it finally hits home that you are in a narcissistic relationship, you must get away from the situation as quickly as possible. You will never ever change the person you are with and you can never make the situation better so cut your losses before you get to hurt. The only person that you have the ability to change is you and you do that by not allowing yourself to be abused by this person.

You are entitled to be treated with dignity and respect. Occasionally, you have to demand it. If you are with a person who is forever putting you down and undermining you, then look at it this way – they do not deserve you.

If you can't make the break, the situation is only going

to get worse. Yes, sure, you will have times when everything is fine but that won't last and things will just get progressively worse. Telling yourself it will change means you are living in a land of make believe; you need to snap out of it and get back to reality.

Narcissists are generally unhappy people deep down and he or she will continue to push that unhappiness on to you if you stay around. The sooner you can walk away the better; the sooner you can begin to recover and move on with your life while he or she gets on with theirs. Don't be surprised to see them turn to someone else immediately; that's what they do. They need to have someone on whom to project their inadequacies and if it can't be you, quite simply it will be someone else.

Do not fall into the trap of missing the good times or envying the new partner those good times. They don't last, as you well know and, if you really think about it, they weren't all that good because of what followed. All of the negativity inside him or her has been dumped on you and, in their eyes; they can start again with a clean slate. It won't take long for that negativity to appear again though, especially if you are seen to purge him or her from your life completely.

The new partner will then become the target for the negative emotions. Look at it this way – the more you grab back the energy you lost, the more you begin to rebuild your self-worth, the less energy he or she has and that's why the new partner becomes the next target. You see, he or she took your energy from you so they could seduce the next target. If you take that energy back, what will they use then? Their new partner's, that's what.

Don't be tempted to sit around and pity yourself. Just because he or she may have a younger, perhaps better-looking model now doesn't mean that you need to continue feeding their energy. If you do, you will never recover fully. It's time to turn your love on yourself. Yes, you may have had some good times and you may have loved him or her once but not anymore. Trust your intuition – it's what told you to leave in the first place and it's what is telling you now that you need a loving relationship, a stable and healthy one.

You opened the door to let them go, now shut it behind them and don't let them in again.

Step 2 – Break All Contact

The only way to break away from a narcissist is to break of all contact with them and that has been proven by many different studies. This means NO contact whatsoever. Delete their phone numbers; change yours if necessary. Delete their email address and have a system in place so that any emails they send you are blocked. If any letters arrive from them, bin them straight away, burn them if necessary but do not read them and do not respond.

Curiosity is a dangerous thing and if you fall foul of it, you are allowing them to control the situation again, which is exactly what they want. Whatever he or she has to say to you is going to be some form of manipulation or anger at you shutting them out.

You are going to ask yourself if they ever really loved you and the truth of the matter is that NO, they did not. Narcissists are not capable of projecting that love on to anyone else. The simple reason for that is that they do not love themselves, not deep down. He or she is spending their entire life hiding from himself or herself and from everyone else and this is why they live in a world of make believe. However, that does not mean that you are an unlovable person because you are. You do need to work on your own self of self-worth and self-love first because a lack of these is what drew you to the narcissist.

When the time comes to cut all contact with the narcissist in your life, you should do it as if it is a matter of life and death. If he or she knows that there is a chink in your armor, that is their way back in. You have to act as though you do not exist in his life, as if you are dead to all intents and purposes. He or she cannot be made aware that you are still there. He or she must be made to feel that you do not care, you never did, and that you are totally indifferent to them.

Indifference is absolutely the worst thing to do to a narcissist but in a good way. If you are still pining for him or her, they have a way in. If you are angry, they have a way in but if you are indifferent, that will hurt them. Because indifference means that you are totally detached, have no emotions whatsoever where they are concerned. And emotion is the food that a narcissist needs to survive.

It doesn't matter if your pain is the worst kind, he or she does not need to know. That pain is between you and your support circle, no one else. If you happen to run across him or her anywhere, push the indifference to the fore. Ignore them; you do not see them. A little trick here to get you started – wear a pair of dark sunglasses on your head. If you see your ex-narcissist, simply put the glasses on and walk on by. If they can't see your eyes, they can't see you and they have no way in.

When the time comes to make that break, write one letter – the last one you will ever write to them. This is your chance for closure so write everything in that letter. Write about how they spend all their time dumping their negative energy on you so now it's time to turn the tables. Send that negative energy right back. Dump on them the way they dumped on you and make sure you say everything you want to say, no matter how mean or nasty. This is the last thing you are going to do and, once the letter is sent, you are going to shut that door forever.

This final part is important –make sure that door is shut and you have removed all avenues of contact. The first thing he or she is going to do is attempt to contact you. Block your emails, block your phone calls, and send mail back unread. This is not your problem anymore; don't let it become one again.

Step 3 – Get Angry

When you have suffered through long periods of abuse,

you should be angry although you may not realize it at the time. You must allow that anger to come out – keeping it locked away will just damage you further and will stop you from healing. And, to deny yourself the right to be angry, well, you are acting in much the same way as your narcissist did.

It is difficult because, when you are in your relationship with your narcissist, you have taught yourself not to show your anger. If you did get angry over anything, you were "out of control" or you were the one that was being abusive and you were told that you needed to calm down. You could have been voicing your opinion of their treatment of you but it would turn around to put the fault squarely on your shoulders. The subject of their abuse would be neatly sidestepped, a highly typical manipulation of a narcissist.

Victims of abuse from a narcissist do not believe they can have a voice simply because they spent so much time under the control of him or her. The only voice you were allowed to have was to positively praise them;

anything about them that was negative would be shut out immediately.

The end result of being kept quiet and not being allowed to show your feelings is one of the worst kinds of depression. This is what your anger will do if you have an outlet for it; it eats away at you and makes you bitter. You cannot allow that to happen because then they have won; not you.

Allow your anger free reign. Express how you feel. That is what the last letter to them is all about – getting angry. If you have already shut down all contact then right your anger down in a letter and then burn it – do not send it because that is opening up the doorway again and that can never be allowed to happen.

Do be careful whom you take your anger out on – it won't do you any good hurting those who are close to you. Go and see a therapist if necessary, that's what they are there for. Use a punch bag, punch your pillow, scream, and throw things. Whatever you do, get all that anger out of your system. You will feel an innate sense of calm afterwards and you will start to feel your energy returning to you.

I must add a word of caution here – if you have been in a long relationship with a narcissist or a particularly intense one, you may be emotionally unstable for a time. You must NOT do anything stupid. Do not let your anger get the better off you and start stalking the narcissist; don't break into his or her house or damage their possessions or, even worse, them! Nothing is worth falling foul of the law for.

Properly expressed, anger is healthy. Work it off in a positive way and get back your sense of self-worth without doing any harm to anyone, least of all yourself.

Step 4 - Grieve for What You Have Lost

Once you have expressed your anger, allow your grief to

come out. You will feel grief, whether it is because you have lost someone you thought was special or because your love has been used and thrown back in your face. It doesn't matter whether they are worth your grief; you are.

Think of it as experiencing a death. The death of your relationship and of the illusion as to what the relationship was. That's right, it was just an illusion, not real, and this is possibly the most painful part you will have to deal with.

Crying is healthy, it helps you to release tension and emotion, and I guarantee that you will feel better after having a good cry. It may not last and you will have to do it again but it will get better. You will be purging yourself from deep inside. There are several stages to grief:

- Denial – the first stage, the disbelief that this is actually happening to you

- Anger – the second stage, where you start to ask, why you, what did you do to deserve this?
- Bargaining – the third stage where you make deals with yourself to get through it
- Depression – the fourth stage where you just can't be bothered with anything
- Acceptance – the fifth stage where everything is going to be just fine and you tell yourself that

It isn't as straightforward as working through the stages one at a time. Most people bounce around and will feel some stages two or three times. You may not even experience the in that order. The important thing is that you do go through all five stages in order to heal and come to terms with what has happened, so you can move on.

However you choose to grieve, do not let it go on for too long. You must start getting on with your life again and interacting with new people even if you really do not feel like it. Once you make that first outing, you will start to feel much better about life and about yourself.

One thing that you can do to make yourself feel better is gather up everything that reminds you of your ex-narcissist and burn it – all letters, mementoes, everything that reminds you of the life you had together.

Do whatever it takes to show your grief, it is an important part of the healing process. It shows that you are human and that you are capable of feeling.

Step 5 – Remove the Psychic Bonds That Hold You Together

Whether you believe it or not, there is an energy web that holds us all together. You can't see it, but it is there. And that energy bond runs between you and the narcissist. More than that, your energy fields have bonded together, they are interwoven and they must be broken otherwise he or she still has access to your energy and to you.

In fact, just by thinking about a person you are letting them in and giving them access to your energy. You must cut the bonds between you and the narcissist in your life. This is important, to stop him or her from feeding on your energy, from using you any further even though there is no longer a physical relationship there.

There is a process you can do to cut those chords. It is simple and you won't see it happening but you will feel it. Before you start, get yourself in the mindset that this is a ceremony of sorts. Light a candle or two burn some incense or some sage and make yourself comfortable, so you are relaxed. Lying down is the best way for this.

Close your eyes and imagine that there is a chord coming from your solar plexus, just above the navel, and it is stretching all the way to the narcissist. You can see it. Now, you have to imagine yourself cutting that chord. Imagine that you have a large pair of golden scissors or a sword. Now cut it at a level with your navel. Take hold of the cut end and direct it upwards towards the sun or down towards the ground. You must do something positive with it so it cannot reattach itself to you.

Now, because you are imagining all of this you can let your imagination take over and run riot here; do what you need to do to end this once and for all. Visualize those ties being cut, See the energy in that chord splitting; yours is coming back to you and theirs to them. Ask him to return to you all that he has taken from you – the pieces of your soul, your heart, and your very being and give back anything that you have taken from him.

Now imagine a brilliant white light is surrounding you. It is providing you with protections and sheltering you from any bad energy that may come your way.

Once the chord cutting ceremony is complete, run yourself a warm bath with sea salt in it. Sea salt is known for its properties in removing negative energies. Just pour half a cup into a hot bath and lay in it for at least 20 minutes.

Remember one thing – it is very easy for those negative

chords to attach themselves back to you if you let the narcissist in, no matter how you do it. You only have to think of him or her and it will happen so you may need to perform this ceremony a few times to be certain the chords are cut forever.

Step 6 – Look after Yourself

When you feel down and a little depressed, it is hard to even think about looking after yourself but this is the very time when you should be. You need to eat properly, get plenty of rest and fresh air, exercise is important as well.

A narcissist will take great joy in watching the people he hates suffer. He will goad every second that he sees you in a miserable state. Do not give him that pleasure. It will only fuel his already inflated ego. Take good care of yourself and enjoy every minute of your life without him in it. Watching you enjoy yourself could tear apart the narcissist and that could be the sweetest revenge you could ever have. If you get lucky, he might miraculously make an effort to change himself for your benefit.

Now is the time to pay attention to you, read the books that you want to read, listen to music, relax in long hot baths and treat yourself – all of the things you couldn't do in the relationship with the narcissist.

One of the most important things is what you eat. Most of the food available to us today is poor quality, full of sugar and the wrong kinds of fat, not to mention chemicals and toxins. These all affect how the chemical balance in your body works, as well as your health and a poor diet has been shown to adversely affect moods as well.

Just making a few changes in your diet can have a significant impact on your wellbeing and on how you feel about yourself. The very first thing to do is remove all forms of processed food from your diet. Anything that has white sugar, table salt, white flour, anything fried or boxed, in a bag or a can. Cut out all convenience foods and fast foods.

If you are used to living on a diet like this, it's going to be tough at first but I promise you will start to feel the benefits very quickly. Plus, an added bonus – having to eat more healthily means preparing more meals from scratch and choosing your ingredients carefully which leads to another place to focus your energy. That leave you less energy to think about the narcissist you left, thus shutting him or her even further out.

When you switch to a whole food organic diet, your body will start reacting straight away. Your body has been crying out for these nutrients for so long and it will repay you in spades for giving it what it needed. Eat plenty of fruits and vegetables, nuts, seeds, whole grains and drink plenty of purified water and herbal teas.

Your body will react by balancing out the chemicals that affect your moods – you won't have the sugar highs and lows and you will feel so much better, both in yourself and about yourself. You will have more positive energy to focus on a new lifestyle, one that does not include being bullied by a narcissist.

Exercise is an excellent way of looking after yourself. Take up yoga, go for long walks, even go to a gym, or join a trampoline club. Not only are you getting fitter you are also releasing negative energy through exercise and replacing it with positive.

Meditating is an excellent form of exercise for someone who has been depressed, or is down and out. Your mind needs time out sometimes and meditation is a good way of clearing your mind of all the negative thoughts. Combine this with deep breathing and your mind, body and spirit will benefit immensely. Do this twice a day to start with until you start to feel better and then you can do it when you feel the need to.

Relaxing in hot sea salt baths is also an excellent way to release negative energy and boost the positive energy. You can also combine this with candles and meditation for the ultimate relaxation experience.

Believe it or not, one of the best ways to look after yourself is to write, on a daily basis, in a journal. It can help you to touch base with your feelings and your emotions. It can also help you to see yourself on an objective basis and see where you need to change things.

Getting out about in nature can be of tremendous help. Nature is one of the biggest healers; along with time, and the more you are in it, the more you will feel its power healing you. Walk in meadows, in the woods, by a river or stream. Just sit and watch the stream, listen to the birds and the other sounds and signs of nature and you will begin to feel an inner peace you thought you had lost, forever.

The most important thing is, no matter how you do it, to take time out for you. Everything I have talked about here needs commitment from you and now is the best time to start looking after you for a change. Put yourself above everything for a time. Buy yourself treats, go for a massage, eat well, and be happy.

Go back to college or night school and learn a new subject. Give your life a meaning again, a new direction. In short, when life gives you lemons do not turn your nose up at them – use them to make lemonade with and enjoy what you have.

Step 7 – Go Out Into the World Again

Hibernating at home, shut away from the world will only serve a purpose for a short time. The longer you stay like that, the harder it will be to face the world again so the sooner you do it, the better. This time, you will step out with your head held high.

You must reconnect with positive people and you can do this in a number of ways. Go to a spiritual growth class to start with; it will help you to bring back that positive energy.

Volunteer at a place that needs you, a cause that needs your help, and one that you believe in. Doing something for others can help you to feel better about yourself and it's a great way to get out and meet new people. Your compassion for other people will show through and you will benefit from the way that makes you feel.

If you find that you cannot do it, you can't take that first step then you may need to consider seeking help in the form of therapy of some kind. Do be sure to find a counselor who specializes in or at least have some knowledge of narcissism and the way it affects victims. They are the only ones who can possibly understand what you are going through and how you feel.

You could look on the internet for support groups for victims of narcissistic abuse; these are people who have been through it or are going through it now and they can be of tremendous help to you.

Fill up your spare time with positive things, go out, see people, and generally get back into the land of the living. Take yourself off to the movies, to a restaurant for a nice meal. Go places where you can meet new people. You could even go on a short vacation to a retreat somewhere. Whatever you, you need to get out from inside your head, especially while you are in the healing phases.

Make a list of all the things you have ever wanted to do. Put them in order of those that are easily achievable down to those that may be more difficult. Now write down what is stopping you from doing these things. Find a way around what is stopping you and do it.

Live your life in ways you have never been able to do before. Get out and be seen. Be heard and take up your rightful place on this earth. Live your life the way you want to and be positive above all else.

Life really is only what you make of it. Forgive yourself for everything that you have done in the past and that includes letting yourself be badly treated and abused. Let go of the past and embrace the future and remember this – it is not your fault. It never was. You cannot win in a relationship with a narcissist; all you can do is break free and walk on.

Chapter 11: Surrounding Yourself With Safety In Order To Survive

As normal people, we have the ability to love anyone we please, as long as we are able to put up with them. For ages, we have cracked the secret of being able to put up longer than expected by learning how to understand our loved ones fully well.

Narcissists, no matter what the type, are continually striving to refine their craft of deception and that includes being normal or blending in. Due to this incredible ability of the narcissists to blend in, getting to spend *quality* time with them and even falling in love with them is not impossible.

We have to anticipate that the newly kindled love story with a narcissist, while in the beginning looks very promising, sweet, and fairytale-like, will soon turn into abusive, painful, and a very unfair relationship. This cannot be avoided, as narcissists are prone to use the *bait-and-switch* technique.

So, what can you do after ending a relationship with a narcissist and deciding to just love them from afar? What should you do so you can get back on track and attend to the wounds that your narcissist ex-lover has inflicted on you?

Normally, when a person is wounded, he or she tries to nurse it. Sometimes, while you are nursing your wound, certain people come to you showing their interest in helping you nurse your wound so you can get back to living life like you should. I understand there would be some sort of trauma here, because of a past experience from a narcissistic ex. But how do you know that this person who just came to you is *safe* and wouldn't hurt you again like how your narcissistic ex did or worse?

In this chapter, we will focus on picking up the pieces and rebuilding yourself after sharing your life with a narcissist. The concept is making sure that you will, from now on, always be surrounded by *safe people.* Of course, nobody wants to be thinking and feeling safe and secured only to realize the next day that all of these feelings are nothing but a mere product of a facade.

1. His Views on Perfection Matters

Considering a person's view when it comes to perfection, about anything, matters a lot. Not only will you be able to protect yourself against narcissists, you will also be able to avoid perfectionists and even obsessive-compulsive people.

If this new person isn't afraid to show you his flaws, while not exactly being proud of them, then you are a step closer to finally being able to share your life in a normal way again.

Remember, this person isn't perfect and after a couple of days or months spent with this person, you shouldn't feel the constant need to be perfect just to make him happy and satisfied.

2. He Should Genuinely Care for Your Happiness

Some people would want you to achieve or gain something because it would mean gain for them as well. You see, it can happen anytime or any day in a scenario that seems very innocent and even sweet.

Say, for example, your boyfriend wants you to be able to get a new car. You have been trying to save your money for a long time, so you can buy yourself a new car. However, you are thinking twice because you know that you can use the money for far more important things.

This is where your selfish and probably even narcissistic

boyfriend comes into the picture. He suddenly starts lecturing you about self-deprivation and kept telling you in a subtle way that you cannot bring your money in the grave with you. That you deserve to give yourself a well-deserved gift and that he only wants you to be happy.

Seems sweet, right? If you tell this little story to someone who barely knows your *boyfriend,* they might even become a little envious and tell you that you are lucky to have a boyfriend like him. However, this may not exactly be the case especially if your boyfriend is a narcissist. How?

You see, you being able to buy yourself a new car can feel very nice, especially if you have enough money to buy yourself a high-end one. A narcissist can benefit from this because, as a partner, he gets to ride in your car too. Imagine the attention a high-end or a cool looking mid range car can get? Now, imagine yourself coming out of that car and imagine a person, a very arrogant one, coming out of it. And I almost forgot, usually a partner can also borrow his or her partner's car. You see how it works, now?

If a person, a *safe* one for that matter, genuinely cares for you, he will want you to gain or achieve something simply because he wants you to be happy. It does not matter if he or she gets to share it with you, just as long as you are happy.

3. He Isn't Going Through the Trouble of Conditioning You To Agree with Him

In short, if this person genuinely cares for you and only wants your companionship, he or she will not manipulate you. There would be no kudos or affirmations that would only turn out to be mere instruments to manipulate you for his or her ultimate benefit.

Yes, there would be affirmations, but those affirmations were given to you by him simply because you deserve it and you really did a good job.

4. Respect is Possible Even Without Equality

A narcissist usually expects everybody else to respect him or her, simply because he thinks he is entitled to this kind of treatment. The problem with this is, once you respect him as he wanted you to do, he will start treating you as his inferior.

The status difference is already a given when it comes to any kind of relationship. This is not new to us anymore, especially if you've had your share of several relationships and lessons acquired from them.

There have been several couples, normal ones, who were able to survive for years and even decades despite the presence of a status difference in their relationship.

Yes, this is definitely possible, but never expect a narcissist to be able to achieve this with you. If a *safe* person genuinely wants to be with you, equality is never a requirement and won't even become an issue just so you can earn his or her respect. Always remember, respect and equality, while they are sometimes interconnected, are two different things.

5. He is willing to share a slice of life by giving way to his partner's mistakes even when he is also affected by the consequences.

As normal people, we have what most of us would like to call selflessness and it develops out of love for our companions. This is a way of showing our partners that we are willing to stretch our boundaries and our comfort zone, in order to give passage for his other half to grow and learn from their mistakes. These mistakes help mold a healthier relationship and it contributes to the patience of each partner towards each other. Mistakes are always present on almost all relationships. These mistakes guide couples onto finding the best way on how to tackle their relationship during difficult times where fights are always inevitable and arguments are present almost constantly. It creates a stronger bond as well as making the couple understand each other like no other people can. Selflessness becomes the result of complete understanding of the other person's weaknesses and flaws that would equate to stronger ties in the relationship. These traits would surely generate and contribute a lot on how a couple would grow and develop.

6. He is willing to give a piece of his own to her without thinking of himself. He is definitely more than happy to give some more without asking anything in return.

As the relationship continues to strengthen, sharing of things to each other is almost always part of it. Such should be the case for a normal and safe person. Sharing physical, emotional and mental matters to one partner is a big factor and a safe partner can easily neglect selfishness in favor of the happiness of the other partner. Sometimes, these things would be difficult for the partner to give because of his emotional or sentimental attachment to it. However, with love and properly molded relationship, a sense of oneness between the two creates another entity which transforms two individuals into one, abolishing selfishness and self-centering a thing of the imagination. This entity creates a lasting tie that would hold a family properly and providing much dedication to pleasing each other with various things. It also helps magnify and amplify the good intents of the partner to another with close observation of what makes one another happy and continuously stimulating it not only for the benefit of the other but also to oneself as well. Being generous is one way of saying such trait and would grow a long way depending on the better understanding of what the wants and needs of each couple.

7. He does not need his partner to get what he wants

Many narcissists are constantly using the act of manipulation and deception in order to force the partner to do what their heart desire. By eliminating manipulation and force insertion of things that can be used to manipulate, it can help to further evolve into proper understanding of needs and wants to each other without a constant reminder and spoon-feeding. Becoming wary and informed of the needs of the partner and what they really want from each other helps eliminate the need to form a scenario where the couple should orchestrate things in order to reach to what they would want from each other. Understanding acts like an invisible rope that connects each other and helps figure out the needs of two individual just by eye contact or body language. This is surely a big factor that could determine how strong the relationship is. Mutual understanding is also a good example of this that makes up a puzzle between the couple that fits perfectly and easily figured out when needed by one of them. It might not work perfectly, but it is always good for relationships where communication and complete understanding would reach better results.

8. He is completely honest with his feelings towards you.

Honesty is a very important aspect that couples need to work on for the relationship to prosper to greater heights. As they say, secrets could ruin a lot of things, and most definitely, relationships included. It is the building blocks of any relationship and if one is transparent and not keeping secrets, the relationship would surely excel better. Relationships with poor communications due to concealment of secrets to one another can create gaps that would later on become potholes where the couple may stumble upon during hard times. When honesty is constantly observed, relationships get to be more progressive and barriers would be removed making it easier for partners to journey through their relationship with ease.

It is also better that the feeling is mutual and practiced by both partners for it to completely work out. It is like rowing a boat with just one paddle. The boat being the relationship would definitely be harder to stir if the other would not paddle in the same direction as the other. Synchronicity is key to making it generate better results and would be easier for both partners to understand how to go about handling situations that would face them along the way.

9. He is more concerned of you overall than of what you are in at the moment

The overall concern for your new partner's overall life and not just about what he is currently on is a sign of a good relationship that guarantees a safe partner and environment altogether. Narcissism is mostly involved on short term sensing, and once a narcissist sees a thing or two that he does not like, he will soon develop an urge to distance oneself to them because of fear of being affected in the process. They are more concerned of what would happen to them that of their partners, so early problems definitely equate to a narcissist escaping it in a complete rush. Make sure to look for signs of overall concern because this definitely means a stronger tie between each other. It simply means that he or she is willing to accept all odds in order to spend time and stay with the other. It also means that he is clearly not narcissist.

Conclusion

Narcissism is affecting more and more people in the world today. If narcissism was a rare case in the past it is on a steady and dangerous rise right now. What makes this rise faster than it should be are the social media that can be found anywhere in the World Wide Web.

It has increased your chances of meeting with a narcissist greatly. Be ready to handle any kind of challenge he might throw at you. If you must live with a narcissist, it is very important that you take appropriate steps to secure your safety. Be prepared for all of his outbursts of rage.

Narcissists can be extremely charming and are master manipulators. So be ready and vigilant for any scam he might try to pull over you. It is easy to lapse into a narcissistic personality nowadays. Taking a few selfies or making a few self-appraising comments on social media need not necessarily turn you into a modern day Narcissus. However, it would be best for your own interests if you kept such interactions to a bare minimum.

No one is going to assess your worth by going through your Facebook or Twitter profile. Keep your emotions intact. Do not drift off into a stage where you don't care about anyone but yourself. Indulging in luxuries may be a necessary addition to certain lifestyles. Make sure that you always value people and relationships above all things material.

On the other hand, it is also important that you visit a psychotherapist together so as to have a safe place where the both of you can communicate through proper channels, and in a safe environment. This is highly recommended because in such an environment he is forced to listen and sometimes it may even work out in your favor. If you choose above all his imperfections and decide that you want to spend your life with him be very careful how you handle him. In case of doubts or if you aren't sure, be sure to seriously consider seeking professional help. If any relationship amounts to physical abuse or mental torture then it is not worth fighting for it anymore. Alienate yourself from such people and start fresh.

It is not a crime to have narcissistic tendencies because in most cases, it is not your fault. Childhood situations and its effects are crucial in shaping a person's character. It can be treated and you can recover to lead a perfectly normal life if you put your heart and soul into it. I wish you the best on your journey to a healthier mental state.

You May Enjoy My Other Books

Author Page

http://hyperurl.co/Jeffdawson

PSYCHOPATH: Manipulation, Con Men And Relationship Fraud

smarturl.it/psychoa

Boundaries: Line Between Right And Wrong

hyperurl.co/boundaries

NARCISSISM: Self Centered Narcissistic Personality Exposed

hyperurl.co/narc

Personality Disorders: Histronic and Borderline Personality Disorders Unmasked

hyperurl.co/borderline

BODY LANGUAGE: How To Spot A Liar And Communicate Clearly

hyperurl.co/bodylang

Tantric Sex and What Women Want - Box Set Collection: Couples Communication and Pleasure Guide

hyperurl.co/sexwomenwant

Boundaries In Marriage: Line Between Right And Wrong

hyperurl.co/marriage

Boundaries: Crossing The Line: Workplace Success and Office Sex

hyperurl.co/crossline

Personality Disorders: Psychopath or Narcissistic Lover?

hyperurl.co/psy

Boundaries: Parents and Teenagers: Sex, Privacy and Responsibility

hyperurl.co/boundariesteens

Made in the USA
Lexington, KY
02 September 2016